First Deceit

BOOK ONE OF THE FATAL DECEIT TRILOGY

Henry Farley

FOR IRENE

CONTENTS

ACKNOWLEDGMENTS

The acknowledgements are growing as I hope my writing skill is growing. The current state of my writing career is down to the following people who have given me encouragement and support.

Belinda Hatton gave me encouragement to finish the novel many years ago.

John Weir made sure I steered a clear course for this type of novel.

At this point, I would like to thank my mentor Alinka Rutkowska of Author Remake, who is trying to get me to think of writing as a business and advising me of the available options and opportunities.

My daughter, Sharon Farley, gave me a good lesson in effective writing, which has led me to revise *Better Dead than Alive* under the new title of *Fatal Deceit* (the title evolved thanks to Alinka). I have had enough feedback to know that the story is engaging, and hopefully, it will now be even more enjoyable.

Rose Miller is a phenomenal cover designer. She did the cover for this book and was able to get quickly to the heart of what I wanted. I hope the readers find the cover as interesting as the story.

Lee Feeney is a friend of mine who has been very encouraging and supportive with his comments. They have helped enormously, particularly during periods of inactivity.

Finally, I have to thank my wife, Irene, who is always there for me, patiently reading my stories and listening to my plans for the future. I use her as a sounding board for everything and she always gives me good advice.

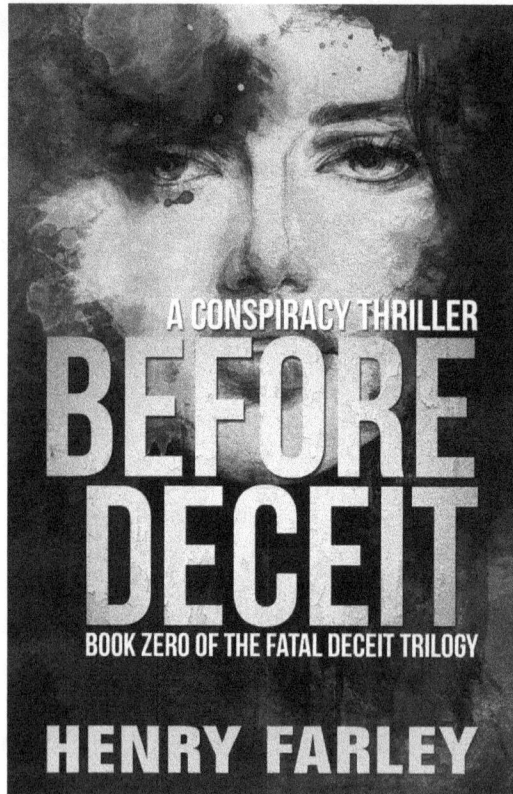

1:

THE PICKUP

Elsa Bartelli could not have foreseen the chain of events that would lead to her premature demise. Her own welfare was the last thing on her mind as she pondered the prospect of making contact with the mark that would provide her and Jack with enough money to quit their unsavory racket and start afresh. She had played this scene so many times she sometimes felt like an observer rather than a participant. Once this business was over, she could return to New York and back to her 'normal life'; the sooner the better.

Elsa had been in Miami for a little more than a week with her lover and 'business' colleague Jack Cates. Jack had read about Simon Walsh, a wealthy businessman, who had taken over the running of the National Mutual Provident following the death of his father Seán. Despite being a married man, Simon Walsh had a reputation as a philanderer, and always spent a couple of weeks alone in Florida at this time of year. As the chief executive of a multi-million-dollar insurance and investment company, his affluence would be a lucrative source of income for Elsa and Jack. Walsh spent his time in Miami sailing and playing golf, and often had a drink or quick bite at the Ocean Drop Inn, a bar and restaurant constructed as part of a marina complex. The complex, including various shops, restaurants and a games arcade, mirrored several similar developments, using diversity to attract customers.

The Ocean Drop Inn boasted a 50-foot bar that was seldom fully utilized, except when regattas or the annual open yacht race were being held. Its decor followed a nautical theme with blue-and-chrome livery and stainless-steel fixtures and fittings. Attempts by the designers to make the furnishings and artefacts authentic only succeeded in making the place look tacky and artificial.

Sauntering into the Ocean Drop Inn, as she had on the previous five days, Elsa positioned herself at one end of the bar where she could easily observe the entrance. Automatically, she opened her handbag, and withdrew a packet of cigarettes. As she was about to put a cigarette to her mouth, she asked the barman if he had a light. He lit her cigarette, using a book of matches, and asked her what she wanted to drink.

"I'll have the usual, Jerry. That's a vodka tonic in case you've forgotten already."

Jerry smiled acknowledging the order. He had seen a number of afternoon drinkers in his time, but none quite like this one. Her manner was presumptuous and tinged with arrogance, and together with her affectation of ordering her drink as if she were a regular, after just a few days was becoming more than a little annoying. Usually, she acted as if she were waiting for someone and her vigil at the bar was short — between 2:00 and 4:30. But she was a good-looking woman; beautiful even. Her stunning appearance was coupled with Mediterranean allure by her dark hair and tanned skin and the faint trace of an Italian accent. She had large, green eyes, high cheekbones and a full, sensual mouth.

"Since you're now a regular, I guess I should ask you your name," said Jerry, handing her a glass of vodka and a small bottle of tonic water.

Jerry took the opportunity to take a good look at her close up. She was dressed like many tourists, but in having a full, rounded figure, she gave the clothes more than a hint of sex appeal. She wore a crop top, shaped around her breasts and cut off before reaching the waistband of her jean shorts that were frayed around the tops of her legs. The clothes gave a good appreciation of her figure, which was shapely and well-toned like a dancer or even an athlete. Jerry saw many different people coming into the bar, mostly in search of a good time and company, but he couldn't think of any reason why she would want to become a regular visitor.

"Names only get in the way," Elsa replied. "We'll become close friends, visit each other's houses, go to the christening of each other's children, and then you'll quit your job. I'll be stuck for someone to talk to when I come to the bar, and end up drinking too much, which can only lead to a bad end!"

Jerry laughed, thinking beauty and wit a rare combination. On top of that, she could hold her drink. She used one bottle of tonic for three shots of vodka, normally having six measures without showing any ill effects from the amount of liquor he had poured for her.

Before Jerry could reply to Elsa, Simon Walsh walked into the bar. Walsh was a keen sailor and had a boat permanently berthed at the marina, though he usually spent no more than a couple of weeks of the year vacationing in Miami. Elsa methodically eyed Walsh up and down as he approached the bar, then feigned disinterest and turned her attention back to her drink. She didn't want to spend another week posing as a barfly — or away from work — and was determined to snare him by drawing his interest. Experience had taught her that the best way of getting a man's interest was to ignore him.

Walsh was not unattractive. He looked over 6 foot, of heavy build and about 10-15 pounds overweight but not fat. The white, cotton shirt and wool-blend, pleated trousers set off his ruddy complexion, and the thick, copper-colored hair betrayed his Irish heritage. On his wrist, he was wearing a Rolex watch that must have set him back $50,000, and his ensemble was completed with black, soft-leather sailing shoes.

"The usual, Mr. Walsh?" said Jerry with a sideways smirk at Elsa.

"Thanks, Jerry," said Walsh as he casually glanced around the bar. The place was virtually empty, apart from Elsa and an elderly couple sitting in the corner, who were nursing their drinks as if they had to make them last all day. Walsh fixed his gaze on Elsa who was an unexpected bonus to his visit. He waited until their eyes met, and smiled, trying not to register too much of an obvious appreciation of her looks. Elsa nodded a polite acknowledgement, then turned back to the bar and sipped her drink.

After thanking Jerry for his drink, Walsh turned his attention back to Elsa, taking in every contour of her body. He considered himself a connoisseur when it came to the appreciation of women, and by any measure, this woman was special. "It seems as if we're the only people here. Can I buy you a drink?" he asked.

Elsa turned back toward him and cheekily replied, "Do you normally check out the number of people in the bar before offering to buy a round of drinks?"

"Sassy too," Walsh thought. "Well, I wasn't counting on buying the couple in the corner a drink, but I can if you want me to show my magnanimity."

"Oh, I wouldn't like you to go out on a limb if the cost of their drinks is going to break the bank."

"Not at all," Walsh replied. "I'm in here waiting for my boat to be refueled and checked over, but I think I should still be able to buy a couple of drinks."

Walsh found it hard to keep his eyes off Elsa's legs. He liked beautiful women and didn't mind spending money on them, as a means to buying their favor. Being the son of a wealthy businessman, he had benefited from the trappings of a privileged upbringing, with a private education and numerous vacations to the most exciting and exotic locations around the globe. Despite this rich background, he still lacked confidence in his ability to attract women with strong personalities and had given up trying to understand them. Now he flagrantly used his wealth to attract any female that caught his eye; their affection was not necessary as long as he was able to get what he needed from the liaison.

"In that case, I'll have another of these," Elsa replied, pointing to her glass, "a vodka."

Thank God things were at last on track, she thought, and he was so easy to catch. He was well and truly hooked, and now all she had to do was reel him in. Jack should be outside somewhere and would follow them to the hotel of Walsh's choice. She would get Walsh into a compromising situation, then Jack would burst into the room as the indignant husband, and bingo — money on tap! It was a well-worn ploy, but worked surprisingly well. The scene would play out like all the others, ending with her being pawed by Walsh before Jack's dramatic entrance, but she was realistic and realized it was the only way she and Jack could get their hands on a large amount of money quickly.

"Have I seen you here before?" Walsh asked, moving toward her and signaling Jerry to fill up her glass.

Elsa shrugged her shoulders, "I've been coming here for a bit of relaxation. It's quiet at this time of day and it's nice just to chill with a drink."

"I know what you mean, but what brings you to Miami?"

"I'm visiting my sister and getting a bit of sunshine. She was able to take time off during the first week, but had to work for the second, so I've been left with having to keep myself amused during the day," Elsa replied, blowing out a cloud of smoke. "I guess the vacation's been a bit flat this week, but that's just my bad luck and timing. I'm actually looking forward to going home tomorrow."

"It's a pity we didn't meet up earlier. I'm on vacation too. I could have shown you around."

"That's OK. I'm familiar with Miami, and know most of what it has to offer. I've visited my sister regularly over the past couple of years, since she moved down here with her job."

"Well, perhaps I could have shown you places that are off the beaten track. I've got a boat out in the harbor. We could have sailed across to the Bahamas."

Elsa gave him a skeptical look and took another sip of her vodka tonic. "Do you always make such generous offers to complete strangers? I'd have thought there would be plenty of people wanting to go sailing with you."

"Only when the stranger is as beautiful as you," Walsh replied. Elsa was taken aback by his sudden directness, but had the presence of mind to acknowledge his compliment. For his part, Walsh wanted to make her aware of his wealth and the material benefits that would be part of any association with him. He had taken the initiative to show he was confidant, even arrogant, which he hoped would pique her interest in him. He was now working outside his normal comfort zone, but he felt that the rewards might be worth the effort.

"Well, in that case, I'd better introduce myself, so I'm not a complete stranger to you. My name is Lisa Millarno," Elsa lied, offering Walsh her hand.

Walsh introduced himself in return, adding that he was the head of a large financial corporation just for good measure. He felt any reinforcement of his wealth and position could only help to increase her willingness to be with him. He desperately wanted to get to first base with this woman and get to know her a lot better. His marriage was flat and uninteresting, and didn't provide a fraction of the frisson he was now feeling during this bar room tête-à-tête.

His own innate insecurities and the coldness of his wife were the root causes leading him to buy the favor of whores, who would satisfy his every whim for the right price. Despite being uncomplicated and very accommodating, they couldn't give him the thrill of the chase and ultimate satisfaction of conquest. Lisa was far more sophisticated than the women he usually slept with, and it was obvious she wouldn't be easily impressed. Despite that, he felt everyone had their price, and it would be interesting to find Lisa's.

"Look," Walsh continued. "I'm about to take my boat for a brief run out to the reef and back. Why don't you come with me? It's fast and comfortable, and there are drinks on board to help us relax and enjoy the sea breezes at the reef. Its range is 260 miles and cruises at 25 knots. Come on! It'll be fun!" he said with a grin.

Elsa feigned uncertainty, but after a brief pause, said, "OK, but I've got to be back at the marina before 7:00."

She was a little uncomfortable about changing the game plan she had agreed with Jack, but hoped that after the sea jaunt, he would be keen to get down to the real action in his hotel. Naively, Elsa didn't think of the problem her partner would have staying on track or the risk she was taking by putting herself in a vulnerable position going out alone with Walsh.

"Relax, there's no problem. Just put yourself in my hands for the rest of the afternoon." Turning to the barman he said, "Jerry give me a bottle of vodka and a bottle of Jim Beam, and put this lady's tab on mine." After Jerry had handed him the bottles of spirits in a take-out bag, Walsh put his free arm around Elsa as they left the bar.

Jerry leaned on the bar and rubbed his chin as he watched the pair exit. That was as smooth a pickup as he'd ever seen. He began to wonder if the woman really was a professional, but she was certainly not the stereotype most people apply to hookers. At least, she had provided a little excitement and glamor just by being there. He looked over at the couple in the corner and asked if they wanted another drink. They shook their heads in unison.

The day was warm and Jack was getting uncomfortable waiting for them to leave as he'd seen Walsh walk from the quayside and enter the bar 20 minutes earlier. He was patient because he knew Elsa would be working her magic, wrapping him around her little finger. Walsh was a step up from some of their other 'clients', and he expected it to result in a big, fat payday. It wasn't easy to walk the tightrope of entrapment, and he hoped Elsa would be able to control him as easily as she had the others. This would be her last scam, and deep down, he wasn't sorry to see it end. The thought of her being mauled by someone like Walsh made his blood curdle.

As they came out, Jack was surprised to see Elsa and Walsh walk down toward the quay. They were talking animatedly, and Elsa looked in control of the situation. In the short walk to the berth where his boat was moored, Walsh took advantage of Elsa in guiding her where they needed to go. Initially, he pressed his hand in the small of her back to control the direction she was taking, but eventually let it rest on her rear. Elsa acted as if she were unaware of his little intimacies, and took his guidance compliantly.

"What are they doing?" Jack wondered as he watched them head toward the berths. It then hit him, as he realized they were heading for one of the boats moored up; they were going out to sea! Suddenly, he began to think he was being complacent in expecting Elsa to handle any situation that confronted her.

2:

FOLLOW THAT BOAT

The day had not started well for Jack. He and Elsa had argued about continuing their search for Walsh. Elsa didn't like hustling for money, and was now so deeply in love with Jack she felt a strong reluctance to peddle her looks and body so cheaply. Jack had tried to argue that she wasn't a hooker and that these types of scam only involved a little cuddling before he stepped in to launch the sting. Jack had only managed to persuade her to go for one last payday by promising this con would be the end. He was convinced that he could wring a princely sum out of Walsh; one that would give them enough to start new lives somewhere else with a totally clean sheet.

His first meeting with Elsa at the Blue Cockatoo nightclub didn't show any signs of them becoming lovers; quite the opposite. Her obvious disdain for the club and its clientele would have been unusual in anyone working in the service industry, but was downright contradictory for a stripper. During the vignettes she choreographed to close the lap-dancing sessions, the audience was engrossed by her presence and the sexual excitement she generated when acting out a scene with a weird combination of arrogance and smut. After several failed attempts by the customers to extend their acquaintance with her beyond the confines of the club, a rumor began to circulate that she was a lesbian. In a male-dominated environment, this only added to her charisma.

Jack was as struck by her exotic appearance and languid body movements as the paying guests. The first time he saw her on stage, she was wearing a white safari blouse and skimpy shorts with a topee and towering, high-heeled shoes, which were a little incongruous with the rest of the outfit but added a touch of spice. Her body was moving sensuously to the drumbeat heard from behind the jungle oasis created on stage. Suddenly, two scantily-clad girls with tiger headdresses jumped into the scene and proceeded to circle and grab at Elsa's costume.

The purpose of the show was to get the girls stripped of their clothes as erotically as possible in their artificial surroundings. It began with the two girls pulling at Elsa's blouse, which had been cut into strips and loosely tied together. The strips started to tear until they barely covered her torso, with her luscious breasts breaking free and causing the audience to cheer with a single voice. Eventually, the tiger girls got her blouse and it ended up as a tug-of-war between the three of them before disintegrating. The act finished with the girls play fighting, but then fondling and kissing each other in simulated sex. The crowd went wild, throwing money onto the stage to keep the girls acting out the scene as long as possible.

Jack could see Elsa was a cut above everyone else, and no matter how cheesy the act, she somehow managed to elevate the mood and impart some artistic merit. Although he would never admit it to anyone, especially himself, it was for him probably love at first sight.

As Jack withdrew from his reverie, he started to follow the pair at a discreet distance. Walsh and Elsa walked to the end of the jetty and boarded what looked like a four-berth sports cruiser. Jack kept his distance, but was able to see the surprised look on Elsa's face as she was helped onto the boat. He took in the size and luxury of Walsh's toy, and began to realize the implications for their scam. Once out at sea, Elsa would find herself alone and defenseless without Jack's protection. He started to panic, looking to see if there were any other vessels berthed nearby he could use to follow them.

Walsh took his position at the controls of his boat, and Elsa sat down on a chair at the stern, casually looking around in an attempt to catch sight of Jack. For his part, Jack wanted to signal to Elsa to get off the boat, but the boat started to pull away slowly from the berth before he could catch her attention. This was a big opportunity, but not at any cost.

Acknowledging he would have to follow Jack thought the change in plan could be fortuitous should he need to get physical with Walsh. Out at sea, he could still play the outraged husband and either threaten to tell Walsh's wife, or to bring a charge of sexual assault to the police. Either way would work, but right now he needed a boat!

Jack quickly walked back to the central area of the wharf to look for somewhere he could hire a vessel. He discovered he couldn't hire a launch or sailboat at short notice and without a skipper, so he hastily looked around the marina, searching for a rank of small motorboats usually hired to people on vacation for fun rides around the bay. Beginning to panic, he spotted a fleet of motorboats on the other side of the wharf and rushed around to the office to hire one. The attendant was still explaining the conditions of hire as he jumped into the boat and turned on the engine. Jack hoped Walsh wouldn't get so far ahead of him that he would lose sight of the sports cruiser. The small boat he had would be difficult to handle if the sea turned rough. Putting the engine into gear, Jack turned away from the wharf to head out of the harbor, and was beginning to think that this was not such a good change of plan after all. By this time, Walsh had negotiated the reverse out of his berth and was already clear of the harbor.

Jack was confident Elsa could handle any awkward situation with Walsh, but she was at risk until he reached her. Another drawback was that he couldn't suddenly burst onto the scene as the sound of his boat would announce his arrival. Jack's concern began to grow as he headed out to sea, and the idea of Walsh forcing himself on Elsa was beyond his comprehension.

Yes, she had handled men like him many times before in the Blue Cockatoo, and had done so effortlessly, but that was in a controlled environment.

She was used to lewd remarks and indelicate touches from her audience during her act, but didn't need to rely on the club's heavies to deter them. She could punch or kick with speed and accuracy and was an expert at the put-down remark, which usually entertained all of the customers witnessing the embarrassment of the wrongdoer. This was a different situation because she was alone and could be overpowered by Walsh, and he, Roland or Frank could not help her.

The sports cruiser looked small on the horizon, and Jack established the direction in which they were headed. Jack eventually felt more comfortable using the motorboat to follow Elsa and Walsh, and even thought he could slow down without putting her at risk. It would give her time to get Walsh into a compromising situation, creating the distraction he would need to sneak up on them. Barging into a hotel room would have been far easier than boarding the sports cruiser because he'd have to manage the awkward difference in height of the two boats.

As he headed after Walsh's boat, Jack drifted back to his earlier reminiscences about his first meeting with Elsa. He had gone to the Blue Cockatoo to visit the owner, Roland Bannister, a qualified legal attorney, who had left the profession for the more lucrative gambling and sex industries in the busy Hell's Kitchen area of New York. He ran a no-nonsense club that provided a safe, secure environment for his customers to relax and enjoy themselves, and didn't tolerate manhandling of the girls. All of the girls looked exquisite, and were under strict orders not to mix with the patrons on the premises. They did offer private lap-dancing sessions, but sexual activity was strictly forbidden, and each room had an alarm button if customers couldn't control themselves. What happened outside the club was their own business.

Girls who had no previous experience before starting work at the Blue Cockatoo were given dance lessons to instill basic movements and timing they could use in their act. Part of the training was through an instruction video of rudimentary routines to reinforce their practice, and after a brief period of rehearsal, they were vetted through auditions before going on stage. Elsa was the best of an excellent group of dancers who had adapted well to the training. She had the advantage of having attended a dance school before working as an exotic dancer.

Jack had provided Bannister with a copy of police records on the disappearance of Leonard Tuzio. Tuzio was a 'made man' with a strong reputation in criminal circles as someone worthy of respect and as a man not to be crossed. He worked for Mario Pallacio, the head of the family business on the East side of New York, whose contacts stretched from New York to the West Coast and right down to Florida. Tuzio managed the finances for the gaming, entertainment and prostitution areas of Pallacio's empire.

Tuzio had first come to the attention of Pallacio after killing a man for the rape of his younger sister; a man who already had a contract on his head for misappropriating lottery funds. Pallacio had Tuzio brought to his office, but instead of punishing him for interfering in his business, he gave Tuzio half of the contract fee for the kill. Pallacio explained that only half the fee was due as Tuzio had a vested interest in the death of the man who had violated his sister. Pallacio offered Tuzio a minor position in his organization to control lottery money. After that, their relationship grew until Pallacio made Tuzio second in command.

Bannister had represented Tuzio on a number of police charges for illegal racetrack betting and prostitution, managing — in some cases, by a narrow margin — to keep him out of jail. Suddenly, Tuzio disappeared following a violent disagreement with Pallacio over peddling drugs to schoolchildren. Tuzio's body was never found, however the District Attorney ordered a thorough investigation of his disappearance in the hope of bringing down his boss. He was unable to gather sufficient evidence to bring charges against Pallacio, and reluctantly, let the matter drop. Tuzio was eventually filed as a missing person.

Shortly after Tuzio's disappearance, Bannister claimed ownership of the Blue Cockatoo with Pallacio's blessing. His story was that he had saved enough money in the short period he had been practicing law to buy a reasonable stake in the club and he had a silent partner who was resident in Jamaica. Jack thought the identity of Bannister's backer must be transparent to everyone, but didn't interfere as he wanted to maintain his friendship with him and retain the use of his club. It was one of the few places in New York that he felt he could relax in safety. If he had too much to drink, Bannister would let him sleep it off in the upstairs apartment.

Jack liked to think that his relationship with Bannister was mutually beneficial. Bannister could use Jack's police contacts in connection with his interests in business ventures and discover if any associated criminal activities that were pending. Although no longer a part of the NYPD, Jack was still well liked and respected and could get information on the status of police investigations or access to their records. They had both cut loose from their earlier professions and went about business with an air of rebelliousness.

Many of Bannister's business colleagues were criminals with police records, and he checked their history from the information Jack gave him to gauge the financial and personal risk of doing business with them. He asked Jack for a copy of Tuzio's file because of pressure from Pallacio, who suspected that he knew of Tuzio's whereabouts. Bannister eventually gave Pallacio a copy of the file that had been slightly modified; it showed that Pallacio was the prime murder suspect, but it couldn't be proven without recovering Tuzio's body. Bannister came to an agreement with Pallacio that he would make sure the police didn't get any leads on Tuzio's whereabouts from anyone at the club, provided he was left in peace. Pallacio pressurized Bannister into taking him on as another silent partner, making it clear he expected a cut from the profits.

Outside his business, Jack was one of the few people Bannister could lower his guard with, and the pair spent many drink-sodden hours reliving old memories and checking out common friends and acquaintances. Jack was popular with the girls at the club, and people who knew him knew of his voracious sexual appetite. He was lucky in that he didn't have to work at it as he just naturally attracted women, partly because he was handsome, but mainly due to his easy-going manner and sense of humor. The casual basis of the friendships formed between Jack and the girls was well understood and accepted by all parties, although Bannister was alarmed at the rate he appeared to be dating the performers, who were sometimes distracted from doing the 'day job' when he was around.

Elsa Bartelli was aware of Jack's reputation as a womanizer, and didn't want to add herself to his list of conquests. She was working at the Blue Cockatoo to make money, and had no intention of mixing business with pleasure. Although few of the clientele looked for artistic merit in her dance routine, Elsa did the job to the best of her ability and added style, flair and technique to the basic bump-and-grind gyrations. Of course, she still had to use the erotic movements required to titillate customers, but her dance training and natural ability allowed her to convey far more sensuality in emotion and timing than the exotic dancing repertoire of the other girls that was limited, but nonetheless was overtly sexual.

Jack saw the seduction of Elsa as a personal challenge, and although he didn't expect to be successful, his ego would not let him give up on the chase. He called her the Ice Queen, and openly accused her of deceit by purveying sexual innuendo without having a sensual bone in her body. The jokes Jack made at her expense antagonized her further, and eventually his desire to get her into bed became a forgotten ambition. The probability of establishing a friendship with Elsa had long passed when a chance meeting allowed him to present himself in a different light and persuade her to change her opinion of him.

Unknowingly, Jack and Elsa had a connection in Queens. As a rookie with the NYPD, Jack had been called out to a disturbance at a café in Queens. A gang of youths had been harassing the owners, Gus and his wife Jean, but they decided to move on after Jack threatened to deal with them individually outside work hours.

Gus and Jean were a friendly couple in their mid-fifties who had opened the diner 20 years earlier, and had continued to serve good basic, no-frills coffee and food ever since. Their diner became a regular port of call for Jack while he was in uniform. After he became a detective, he still visited them often, and enjoyed listening to the stories of their lives together as hippies in the 1960s. On one of his unannounced visits he ran into Elsa, who had once worked as a waitress for them. They pretended to be friendlier than they actually were for the sake of Gus and Jean, although Elsa was concerned that Jack would try to score points by making oblique references to her dancing at the Blue Cockatoo.

Jack made the most of the situation, which allowed him to pretend to be a close friend of Elsa's, much to her chagrin. Out of consideration for Gus and Jean, she was forced to respond to him in a much friendlier manner than he was used to at the club. She was always far nicer to Frank and even Roland than she was to him. The chance meeting gave them a shared confidence, creating a certain equable intimacy between them that had previously been absent.

They left Gus and Jean together, and Elsa thanked Jack for being discreet about her job. She explained that she had worked at their café while training to be a dancer and on leaving she had told them she had joined a touring dance troupe. Jack listened intently and took the chance of asking her to have dinner with him. Elsa reluctantly agreed because she felt she should reciprocate his kindness in supporting her while they were at her former workplace. During dinner, Elsa discovered that there was more to Jack than the stereotype image she had formed of him from their brief conversations, his taunts and the lurid gossip she had overheard among the other girls at the club. When she spoke, he listened, and that encouraged her to tell him more, because there was no one she could take into her confidence. She never spoke to Julie about her emotions because it would soon become gossip at the club.

It had been a long time since she had opened up to another person, and she found the experience rejuvenating. She spoke about her aspirations to be a professional dancer and the difficulty in financing herself through dance school. She was easily able to manage the dancing classes but struggled with the theory, because of her limited education, which was brought about by the need to help support her aging parents; she was too embarrassed to admit she needed extra tuition to improve her literary skills.

The dancing came naturally to Elsa, who had all of the qualities necessary to become a professional dancer — a strong core, flexibility and good balance and timing. The pressures of the written elements of her course began to build, and she eventually dropped out of school because she didn't have the time to make up the shortfalls in her poor education. She now felt her childhood dream had passed her by and that she was too old to break into legitimate dancing, hence she was now at the Blue Cockatoo and getting far more money than she would as an unskilled worker. Initially, she had found it difficult to take her clothes off in front of strangers, never mind perform the sexual movements her routines demanded. If nothing else, Elsa was a survivor and she soon came to understand that she could either allow herself to become intimidated by the leering onlookers or learn to control them using her obvious sexual charisma. She now wanted to make sufficient money to train as a dance teacher, but knew that the first hurdle would be becoming skilled in reading and writing.

As she spoke, Jack began to see Elsa differently. In a strange way, her looks detracted from her as a complete person, as she had many more qualities than those on display. She had far more to offer than her face and body, and through their conversation, she had shown she was emotionally strong and determined to get what she wanted in the best way she could. Underneath the veneer of strength, she was vulnerable, and she had felt alone since the death of her parents. They had Elsa late in life, and during their latter years, relied on her more and more, leaving her no time for herself. Eventually, they both developed dementia, and Elsa needed to hire home help, but they deteriorated rapidly and both died within a few days of each other. After their 60 years together, Elsa was convinced they couldn't live apart.

The only way Elsa had been able to pay for the care of her parents was her work for Gus and Jean, together with the help they gave her when she found herself short of money. They supported her when she needed it most, and now Gus and Jean were her only close friends as she didn't mix with the girls at the club. Her isolation and loneliness grew as she could only visit their café infrequently so as to live her lie as a dancer with a touring troupe. She spoke from the heart and didn't realize Jack was being drawn to her spirit far more than her body.

Jack had stepped through a door into a world different to the selfish, ego-serving reality he had been living in prior to this and began seeing her as a person for the first time. For him, it was a feeling that was new and strangely liberating because now he knew he wasn't obliged to play the mating game with her. All he had to do was be himself and hope that Elsa liked what she saw.

Their relationship grew after this first meeting, and Jack often walked Elsa back to her apartment after she had finished work at the club, much to the annoyance of Julie, who hadn't been given the same consideration. One night, Elsa invited Jack back to her apartment over a weekend when Julie was out of town. He had imagined making love to her many times but the reality was even better than the fantasy. He felt loving and protective and wanted to give her pleasure rather than concentrate on his own gratification. Elsa found Jack a gentle and considerate lover, and tried not to think of him honing his art through his experience with the other girls at the club. His hands and mouth roamed over her body stroking, caressing and teasing, and brought her from one crescendo to another. As he thrust against her, she covered his face and chest with kisses in synchronicity with his movements; she was lost in the moment.

Jack was still daydreaming when he thought he heard the faint but unmistakable sound of a gunshot. He switched off the engine of his motorboat and listened intently. Within a minute, he heard the shrill sound of gunfire pierce the still air again, followed by the loud pulsating throb of Walsh's sports cruiser heading back to the harbor at full throttle. The scream of the engine broke the silence, as the boat passed Jack, creating bow waves that caused his small craft to rock violently. Assuming Walsh was at the helm, Jack thought he must be in a panic about something to act so erratically.

Dormant fears resurfaced as Jack instinctively feared that Elsa must have been hurt or worse. He reached for the binoculars that were supplied with the boat and turned to look at Walsh's sports cruiser, focusing on the rear of the boat as it was disappearing into the distance. He could see the back of Walsh's head at the wheel, but there was no sign of Elsa.

Jack had to make a decision either to follow Walsh or head out to sea. It was difficult to determine the exact direction the gunshot sounds had come from, but he turned on the engine of his motorboat and headed to the point on the horizon he had last seen Walsh's boat reappear. The thought of finding Elsa's body floating in the water made Jack feel nauseous. He stiffened and swallowed unconsciously to prepare himself for the worst.

3:

IN THE WATER

Elsa was more than a little disorientated by the speed with which Walsh took her from the bar to his boat, and started its engine to set off to find an offshore reef. The boat was a lot grander than she had expected and the deck had more space than some of the hotel rooms she'd been in. Her error in judgement was becoming transparent, and she realized that she would have to handle Walsh carefully to avoid getting into an unpleasant situation, and not give any impression she was interested in him in any way. She hadn't seen Jack and didn't know if he was aware of this unexpected change of plan. Becoming slightly anxious, she hoped he had seen what was happening.

Walking along the quay and down the jetty to Walsh's boat, she had tried to catch sight of him, but in her uncertainty as to the direction they were going and her growing anxiety, she was unable to spot him. Jack was a professional she thought, and would only be seen when it suited him, so despite her vulnerability, she didn't envisage any problems, and was sure she could fend off Walsh if he tried to get amorous. She knew Jack would recognize her danger, and find a way to follow, although he would have to be a little more resourceful than usual. Nonetheless, she was aware he couldn't come rushing to her rescue as he had in the past, and she felt isolated as they headed for the boat.

Walsh had swiftly dealt with the mechanic maintaining and refueling his boat and disembarked. He was eager to be alone with Elsa so that he could express his feelings more openly and in private. As he manned the controls, he began regaling Elsa with statistics of the boat's performance capabilities, hoping to impress her with his knowledge and the obvious size and luxury of the vessel. The boat was elegant with aerodynamic lines to reduce the resistance of the water. There were numerous timber embellishments, and the trims were all stainless steel, including handrails and door fittings. The seated area above the aft cabin comprised highly-polished timber framework holding red, leather cushions.

"We'll go out to the reef, drop anchor, have a few drinks, and enjoy the scenery. I know a great spot for seeing the most glorious sunset that isn't too far away," said Walsh, turning back to see Elsa sitting comfortably on one of the deck seats. "There's a good selection of wines on board if you fancy a change from your normal tipple," he continued. Elsa had already downed the equivalent of four shots of vodka at the Ocean Drop Inn. The bar was renowned for the generosity of its shots, which were more like doubles than singles. Walsh's strategy was to continue plying Elsa with drinks to get her a little more relaxed and into the right mood after they dropped anchor at the reef. He didn't think it would be long before she drank enough liquor to allow him to be confident in making a move on her without the risk of rejection. The thought of having sex with her gave him an erection, and he could feel himself flush.

With her anxiety level gradually rising, Elsa said, "I don't want to spend too much time on this boat trip, because I promised my sister I'd be back before 7. She's booked a table for dinner tonight. This is my last night in Miami, and she wants to treat me to a slap-up meal."

"Don't worry! We have plenty of time, so just relax and enjoy yourself. It's a pity this is your last day. Otherwise, we could have spent all day sailing tomorrow," Walsh replied, reaching a high level of excitement as they neared their destination. "Let me know the next time you plan to visit your sister, and I can arrange a short vacation so we can really put this tub through its paces, and have some real fun!"

Elsa sensed Walsh was already expectant of having a close friendship with her and she knew things would get out of hand if she didn't handle him in the right way. She thought it would be best to act cool and distant to terminate the trip as quickly as possible, get back to the marina, and forget about trying to compromise Walsh. It was stupid not to see the situation she was placing herself in from the outset, but she was determined not to allow Walsh to take advantage of her. Men like Walsh were predictable in the way they tried to seduce women, without charm or any subtle nuances that could catch her off guard. The instant he tried to become more intimate, probably in a clumsy attempt to grope her, she would act outraged, but retain her politeness in asking him to return her to the marina. He was a big man and she hoped he would be too embarrassed to do anything more than what she asked. There would be some unpleasantness, but she thought she might be able to stall Walsh by arranging some future rendezvous.

"Don't forget I have to change before meeting my sister," Elsa added.

She could see Walsh was ignoring any suggestion of returning to the marina, determined that they would spend time together.

As the boat approached the reef, Walsh throttled back the engine and coasted into position alongside it. He switched off the engine, pressed a button on the control panel to drop the anchor, then turned to Elsa. "Let's have a drink," he beamed and produced the bottle of vodka given to him by Jerry. He got two glasses from the galley, and poured Elsa a generous measure.

"Not so much!" she said. "Are you trying to get me drunk?"

"Don't be afraid of having a drink. I can take you to where you want to meet your sister so you don't have to drive yourself.

It's your last day on vacation. Just relax and chill out," he replied, pouring himself a much smaller measure of vodka.

"Believe it or not, I usually come out here by myself. I've had parties on the boat, but not as many as you might think. I just love this spot. I hope you do too."

"It's certainly beautiful and tranquil; not like downtown Manhattan, which is the complete opposite of tranquil," Elsa answered.

"I live in New York as well. That's a nice coincidence."

"That's good," Elsa replied, not knowing how to use this information to help her in her current situation.

"We could meet up and spend time together," Walsh continued.

"That sounds like a good idea, but I really have to be getting back soon. Obviously, I'll need to change my clothes before I meet my sister," Elsa reiterated.

"Don't worry! We should get to know each other a little better. That will help when we meet later," said Walsh, disregarding her request. "What do you do for a living?" he added, moving closer to her.

"I work for a financial company as a legal secretary," Elsa lied. "It's not very exciting, but the pay's good and I sometimes get to travel."

Walsh looked her up and down, "It must pay very well judging by the fact you've come here at the height of the season and because of the brief, but expensive, clothes you're wearing. I can see from their quality they're not dissimilar to the clothes my wife buys, so they must be from designer houses."

The clothes Elsa had picked were of good quality; not the usual garments worn by tourists. She also wore some expensive items of jewelry, and had examined herself in the mirror before leaving the hotel room to be sure that she was projecting the right image without being slutty.

"Your wife must be a woman of taste," Elsa replied dispassionately.

"She's able to show off the clothes she has because I buy her everything she needs. Do you have someone who's able to do the same? I don't want to get too personal, and I'm not complaining, because you look great."

"No, I do my own buying. I take care of the way I look because it makes me feel good," Elsa replied, and added, "and that means buying expensive clothes. They also last longer and keep their shape. You would know that too being able to buy designer clothes yourself."

"That's true. You're obviously someone who enjoys and appreciates the good things in life, and I could help you get them." Walsh paused to let his words sink in. Elsa made no response to his offer, and Walsh took her silence as her approval for him to continue. "I come down here often and try to mix business with pleasure whenever I can. I work hard and like to play hard, especially if I can enjoy myself with someone I like and respect." He immediately devalued the sincerity of his last sentiment by putting his hand on Elsa's knee.

"Do you think your wife would approve of this?" said Elsa with outward calm but inward apprehension.

"Do you really care?" Walsh countered, moving his hand to the inside of her thigh. "Forget about my wife, your sister or anyone else while we're here together. Relax! Let's have a good time! Don't worry! I'll make it worth your while."

Walsh's hand was becoming more intrusive as he gained confidence at the thought of Elsa succumbing to his offer. He began kissing her on the neck, and with his free hand, cradled her back and pulled her toward him.

Apart from feeling isolated and vulnerable, Elsa was starting to get irritated at the liberties Walsh was taking and his assumption that she was now ready to accept his advances. She wondered how the hell she had let herself get into such a mess, and she knew she couldn't rely on Jack to come to the rescue because of the speed and aggression of Walsh's assault.

"Slow down, Simon, before we get into a situation we may both regret later," she said, pushing Walsh away.

Walsh was unperturbed, "We're not kids, Lisa," he replied, continuing to stroke the inside of Elsa's thigh. "Whatever happens, you won't be sorry. As I said, I'll make it worth your while, so no one loses. I'm a rich man, and can get you anything you want; anything!"

"That's the same as paying for the use of my body," Elsa retorted, moving his hand away from her leg again. "I don't care how rich you are! I'm not a prostitute!"

"We all have to prostitute ourselves in one way or another, honey, so don't be so damn self-righteous. Anyway, you didn't display such sensitivity in the Ocean Drop Inn, and the way your clothes cling to your body says you don't mind showing off what you've got," Walsh replied, suddenly becoming more assertive in his tone of voice and body language.

"He's not going to be reasonable," Elsa thought, bracing herself for a fierce onslaught. The situation had passed the point where she could handle him with cool politeness, so she would now have to match his aggression to assert herself firmly. "Don't take me for granted, hot shot! It takes more than a few drinks and a boat ride to get inside my pants," she replied, standing up to get away from his continual pawing.

"Hey, what's your game, then? You come onto me in the bar and then play hard to get. What's so special about you? Surely, you can't be saving yourself for Mr. Right."

"No, I'm not waiting for Mr. Right, as you put it, but that doesn't mean I'm willing to have sex with someone I've only known for a couple of hours, no matter how rich they are," Elsa retaliated.

Walsh stood up suddenly in a reflex action to her stinging remark and slapped her across the face. The power of the blow knocked Elsa to the deck, momentarily stunning her. Walsh immediately dropped down on top of her, and tried to lift up her top, ripping off some decorative buttons in his frenzied rage. He moved on to her bra as Elsa began to recover her senses, attempting to push Walsh away without success. Roughly, he grabbed her wrists and pinned them above her head. He straddled her body with his legs to hold her more securely, and tried to kiss her fully on the mouth. Shaking her head furiously, Elsa managed to avoid his mouth. Frustrated, Walsh tried to trap her face with his, raising himself on his knees and bending forward. As he lifted his body off hers, Elsa brought up her knee sharply into his groin.

Walsh cried out in pain, and rolled off her. "You fucking bitch," he screamed, trying to control the numbing pain slowly but inevitably building in his groin. Elsa jumped to her feet and tried to circumnavigate Walsh to get to the controls of the boat and fire the engine. As she turned the ignition key, Walsh grabbed her by the hair, pulled her away from the controls and slapped her again. This time she saw the blow coming, and with dancer's timing, was able to ride the force, and simply staggered backward.

Walsh reached downward to a compartment next to the main console and pulled out a handgun. "You fucking bitch," he repeated, sucking in his breath to control the pain. He cocked the hammer of the gun, and fired it recklessly in Elsa's direction.

"Don't be so stupid!" she screamed, holding her hands out as if to try and stop the bullet. She moved away from him until she was backed up against the rails of the boat. "Nothing's worth murder," she tried to reason with him.

"You're not so superior now," said Walsh, regaining his composure and walking toward her as the pain in his groin subsided. "This gun says you're going to do whatever I want however I want, and thank me after I'm done." Walsh was standing right in front of Elsa, staring straight into her eyes and sticking the nozzle of the gun into her stomach.

"Please, can't we talk this over? We've got off to a bad start, but I can't do what you want without feeling something for you. If our friendship develops, I'm sure I could be really good to you. Listen, I don't want to die out here, so just put the gun down, and we can go back to where we started," she pleaded.

"I know you'll be good to me, you slut, because if you're not, I'll blow a hole in your head, and fuck you when you're dead."

With that, he grabbed a handful of hair at the back of her head with his left hand and pulled her face toward his. He forced his tongue into Elsa's mouth, and he moved the nozzle of the gun down her body and between her legs. The top of Elsa's shorts had opened during her fight with Walsh, and he pushed the nozzle of the gun inside them, rubbing against her through her panties.

Choking under the force with which Walsh's tongue pushed into her mouth, Elsa bit hard on it and pushed him away with all the force she could muster. As he was propelled backward and fell, Walsh tensed and involuntarily fired the gun in a reflex action. The impact of the bullet knocked Elsa overboard.

Startled by the unexpected sound of the gunshot, Walsh stared at the gun in his hand, unable to believe what had just happened. His mind could not handle the shock of Elsa being hit by the bullet, and he feebly staggered to his feet, stumbled across the deck to the rails of the boat and began to look for her in the sea. It had happened so quickly he couldn't comprehend if Elsa had actually been shot, because he couldn't remember seeing if the bullet had hit her. How could this have happened after things had started so well? Once again, he had let the beast within him take control of his behavior. He still treated all women like prostitutes and became unreasonable when they didn't do what he wanted.

Frantically, he scanned the waves for any sound or sight of movement in the water. The light was fading and it was becoming more difficult to focus on any movement in the sea in the twilight. As he searched, a panic set in as the consequences of what had just taken place started to dawn on him. Turning away from the water, Walsh paused to consider his options. If he found the girl and brought her back, she might end up charging him with attempted rape. There would be evidence of their fight from bruising on her face and body.

He was beginning to feel more anxious about the furor that would result from police charges than about Elsa's welfare. She could swim back to the marina he thought, but she would have to be one hell of a swimmer. If she did make it back under her own steam, she would definitely go to the police just to get back at him, and then he would be accused of attempted murder. The odds on her drowning had to be much greater than on surviving, he thought, especially as she was probably wounded.

As the heat of his fight with Elsa subsided, Walsh concluded that fishing her out of the water and bringing her back would only cause him big trouble. He picked up her handbag from the deck and tossed it into the water after her. He then walked over to the control panel, and despite the shaking of his hand, managed to switch on the engine. Opening up the throttle, he turned the boat to head back to the harbor without as much as a backward glance. His temperament had led him into similar altercations with women in the past and he always justified his actions by thinking it was because they didn't meet their part of the deal. The adrenaline in his body, built up during his fight with Elsa, began to ease as he distanced himself from the reef. It was a long way back to the marina and he hoped she'd be unable to swim the distance. There was always the chance the sharks would get her!

4:

WHERE ARE YOU?

Jack was getting progressively more anxious about Elsa's wellbeing as he headed in the general direction of the point on the horizon that Walsh's boat had come from. He knew that trying to find her in the water would be virtually impossible, and he would rather have had the task of trying to locate her in the seedy underbelly of New York. The sun was beginning to set and he could see that the daylight would soon fade. If Elsa was out there in the water, he would have to find her quickly. A sudden panic gripped him, thinking he might not be able to see her in the dim light, and he began shouting her name frantically as he weaved through the water.

As he was shouting, Jack began to worry about the possibility of the noise of the engine drowning any shouts for help from Elsa, or of accidentally hitting her with the hull of the boat. Distraught, and not really knowing what was the best thing to do, he switched off the engine and let it glide through the water. A growing silence succeeded the noise of the engine until all he could hear was the lapping of the water against the hull of the boat. His agitation was replaced by a deep, hollow despair that rose from the core of his soul and manifested itself in an ache in his chest and abdomen. Taking control of his emotions, he pulled himself up from his downward spiraling fears and began calling Elsa's name again, praying to catch some sign of her as he scanned the water. As the sound of his voice died, it was replaced once more by the lapping of the water.

Jack restarted the engine and began weaving the boat through the water again, albeit at a much slower speed than during his earlier attempts to find her. He spotted a reef 40 yards in the distance and again cut the engine of the boat, and glided toward the reef. As the noise of the engine faded, he was again greeted by the sound of the seawater lapping on the side of the boat. He resumed calling Elsa's name without any response. A chill overcame Jack as the possibility of Elsa's death became more and more of a reality, and he began to feel the bile building in his stomach. If Elsa was dead, he was to blame. He had talked her into helping him with the scams, and she was the one at the sharp end of the action, receiving all of the unwanted attention from the would-be adulterers. Jack buried his face in his hands, and he began to sob, regretting every conniving con that had led to this moment.

Suddenly, the silence was shattered. "Don't just sit there! Help me out of the water!" Elsa shouted, grabbing the side of the boat.

She looked bedraggled and weary from floundering around in the sea for the last three quarters of an hour, but at that moment, Jack thought she had never looked more beautiful. He put his hands under Elsa's armpits to pull her into the boat. As he took the weight of her body to lift her out of the water, she gasped in pain.

"Be gentle! The bastard shot me!" said Elsa, half smiling at Jack, who, on seeing a red mark on her shoulder, readjusted the position of his hands to reduce the pressure on her injury.

Elsa could not help him much in her weakened state, and although Jack tried to be as careful as possible, she cried out again from the pain of being manhandled.

Once she was safely in the boat, Jack dropped to his knees, cradled Elsa's head and kissed her firmly on the mouth. The overwhelming sense of relief he felt in finding her alive was unlike any emotion he had ever experienced before. The unbearable tension, which had spread over his entire body earlier, evaporated, and suddenly, with an overwhelming sense of relief, he felt very tired. As he moved his hand to Elsa's right shoulder she winced in pain from its weight. In the half-light, Jack saw the bullet hole through Elsa's crop top and pulled it down off her shoulder to see where she had been hurt. The bullet had made a crease in the top of her shoulder just above the collarbone. The red crease looked deep, but the salt in the water had cleaned the wound. Jack pulled Elsa close to him, trying to comfort her and ease the distress she must have felt while she was in the sea.

"The bastard tried to kill me," Elsa whispered, unable to comprehend fully what had happened to her.

Relief at being rescued was followed by a loss of energy, and she lay in the boat exhausted after believing that she was going to drown. Suddenly, she grasped hold of Jack tightly, and started to cry, allowing her emotions to pour out of her now that she was safe.

"The bastard shot me," she sobbed repeatedly. She then added, "I was thrown overboard into the water. When I realized what had happened, I was afraid he would take another shot at me if he saw me bobbing on the surface, so I swam underneath the boat. Then he started the boat's engine and almost dragged me into the propeller. I've never been so scared. I was certain I was going to die!"

"Don't worry, baby! He's going to pay for hurting you. He's going to pay dearly," Jack replied.

If Walsh had been in his grasp now, Jack would have snapped his neck like a twig. The anger he felt would soon subside once Elsa was safely onshore and on the road to recovery, but Jack wanted to keep hold of the rage he felt so he could use it for future motivation in planning the downfall of Walsh. He looked down at Elsa, who was now comfortably resting her head on his chest. Her wound was still weeping a little but the seawater had helped start the healing process, and there were no signs of excessive redness from infection by the water. He took out the first-aid kit on the boat, and put some antiseptic cream on her wound, but felt it was better to leave it open to dry quicker.

Jack took off his jacket, folded it, and placed it under Elsa's head to make her feel more comfortable lying along the clear length at the back of the boat behind the driver's seat. He then put the key in the ignition and started the motor before turning to check once more on Elsa, who was now asleep. Satisfied that she was comfortable, he put the engine in gear to head back to the harbor. He looked at Elsa again and wondered what kind of man would resort to killing someone because they refused his advances. Nothing could have justified such a blackhearted act. He wanted to make Walsh suffer physically as well as financially, but the best and most lasting way to hurt him was through his pocket. The stakes had risen sharply because Walsh, not knowing if Elsa was dead or alive, could now be blackmailed for attempted murder......or even murder itself. Jack shivered again as he realized how close he had come to losing Elsa, and he opened the throttle of the engine.

By the time they got back to the harbor, the sun had set and the daylight had all but disappeared. While taking the motorboat back to the marina, Jack had put together the framework of a plan to get even with Walsh. He looked down at Elsa sleeping. Her hair was stuck to the side of her face and her eyes were stained from the running of her makeup and puffy from crying. He gently woke her as the boat pulled up to the jetty. "Do you think you'll be able to get to the car park while I return the boat keys and binoculars?" he asked.

"Of course, I will," she replied, feeling uneasy but not wishing to make too much of a drama of her assault. She shivered, and held her hand out for the car keys, clutching the edges of Jack's jacket, which was draped around her shoulders, with the other hand to keep herself warm. Jack felt bad at letting her walk back to the car on her own, but he didn't want to risk her being seen by the motorboat attendant, or anyone else who might still be hanging around the marina.

As he walked into the office, he saw the attendant slumped in his chair, reading a periodical. The man folded the magazine and stood up as Jack reached the counter.

"That was some joy ride you had!" he said. "I was getting ready to call out the coast guard. Didn't I tell you that you were not to go outside the perimeter marked by the blue buoys? These boats should not be taken into deep water. They can't handle big waves."

"I'm sorry," Jack replied. "I lost my bearings, and the time just seemed to fly by. I didn't think I'd gone out too far until I lost sight of the marina."

"You've been out for a long time and you've probably drained the tank. It's a wonder you didn't end up stranded out there," the attendant retorted. He was not going to be placated by Jack's lame apology.

Jack took two $100 bills from his wallet and put them on the counter together with the boat keys and binoculars.

"I hope this compensates you for your inconvenience," said Jack, trying to appease him.

The attendant shrugged his shoulders, picked up the boat keys and dropped them into a drawer behind the counter. Jack smiled and left the office. Watching Jack walk away from the office, the attendant picked up the two $100 bills, and put them in his pocket. His eyes remained fixed on Jack as he made for the exit to the car park. He couldn't remember a woman getting into the boat when he hired it to him, which made him wonder how and where she had gotten onto the boat, and why she looked so unkempt. Whatever her experience, he could tell it had taken a lot out of her by her unsteadiness walking.

As Jack walked back to his car, he felt confident that the attendant wouldn't make a fuss about the late return of the boat, especially as he was $200 better off for a little overtime. When he got to the car, he found Elsa fast asleep in the passenger seat, the keys were in the ignition. He opened the driver's door, got into the car, and started the engine. Elsa stirred a little, but wasn't going to be roused until she had to get out of the car. The vehicle pulled out of the car park and disappeared into the night.

As Jack drove back to the hotel, he worried about the mental trauma Elsa might suffer over the next few days when remembering or dreaming about being shot, and how close she came to drowning. He had no doubts about her physical recovery. Elsa was strong and would quickly bounce back from her ordeal, especially as he would get Doc Brandt to patch her up. Yes, Elsa was resilient, he mused, although he still couldn't help but wonder how easily she would cope with the news of her own death.

Elsa was extremely tired when they got back to the hotel, suffering the shock of her traumatic experience. Jack asked the reception clerk for a wheelchair before collecting Elsa, saying it was for his mother who was visiting him. Elsa was wrapped up in his coat and a car blanket as he passed through reception. "I'm taking her home later, but she needs help getting around nowadays."

"Does she live in Florida?" the clerk asked.

"Yes, she retired here about 20 years ago."

Elsa didn't fully understand the need for the subterfuge, but played along as always.

5:

BAD HABITS

Simon Walsh got back to his hotel at 7:30 p.m. He had a penthouse suite at the Sheraton on Marine Drive that overlooked the beach. He preferred to stay at the hotel rather than on his boat at the marina because it was nearer to the night spots. Still feeling edgy and irritated after the incident with Elsa, he poured himself a large glass of Jim Beam, and found that as he lifted the glass to his mouth his hand was visibly shaking. He put the glass to his mouth, took a large gulp of the whiskey, and swallowed hard. The whiskey steadied his nerves, and he sat down on the sofa cursing Lisa, rather than himself, for his current predicament. The stupid bitch had brought it on herself by stringing him along and then playing hard to get. He shrugged, took another swig of whiskey and decided that prick teasers like that deserve all they get.

But wait! She had a sister, who would now be wondering why she hadn't returned home, or met her at the marina. He didn't know where they were supposed to meet and who her sister would be talking to in trying to find her. Common sense told him that Lisa's sister would eventually realize that she was unable to make their meeting and would go to the police to report her disappearance. Walsh tried to remember Lisa's surname and picked up the local telephone directory and began rapidly thumbing through the pages. His mind was racing as he scanned the pages trying to find Millarno. Unable to concentrate and focus his thoughts on the task, he threw down the phone book, picked up his glass of whiskey, and took another large gulp. The sharp bite of the liquor snapped him out of his agitated state and he became calmer as the numbing effect of the alcohol soothed his brain.

He stared vacantly at the wall directly in front of him and smiled to himself at having another panic attack and at this fit of anger. If by a miracle he did contact Lisa's sister, what on earth could he possibly say to her and how would it help to disguise his part in her sister's disappearance? It would only serve to draw attention to him, rather than deflect it away. Lisa's sister was probably unaware of her sibling's movements during the day, and certainly, wouldn't know of her meeting him and their boat trip together. Mentally, Walsh began to reconstruct the events of the day, trying to identify any one factor that could incriminate him. The only people who could connect him with Lisa were at the marina, and no one had a complete picture of their movements during the time they spent together.

Walsh guessed that hundreds of missing-person reports would be lodged with the police each year. They couldn't possibly investigate every case, and wouldn't have any particular reason to go out to the marina. Jerry had seen him leave his bar with Lisa, and Joe, who maintained his boat for him, saw them sail out of the harbor together, but neither man knew her name, or would have reason to connect Lisa's disappearance to him. He had spoken to Joe about cleaning the boat, but it was a brief instruction made in passing as he left the marina, and the mechanic hadn't reacted to Lisa not returning with him. It was likely that the woman would just become another police statistic. Walsh concluded that the best way of protecting himself from prosecution would simply be to ignore the whole incident and not do anything that could link him to her.

Despite logically trying to think his way out of his predicament, Walsh couldn't forget the shooting or stop worrying about the chance of being charged with her murder. Reliving his fight with Lisa, he couldn't understand how the gun had gone off or the freakish way in which the bullet had hit her. God knows he had no intention of killing her;

he only intended to frighten her enough to get her to agree to do what he wanted. He decided that in future he would avoid unnecessary complications, and stick to dealing with prostitutes. They knew what their clients wanted, and like any other commodity, could be had for the right price. They didn't act as if they had something special between their legs, and if he stuck with the high-class girls, they could be every bit as attractive and alluring as women like Lisa. He poured himself another large glass of whiskey and sat back down on the sofa, now more relaxed than when he had first returned to the hotel.

In his relaxed and now drowsy state, his memory took him back to a comparable incident with a teenage whore in a New Orleans brothel. Unlike most of the sluts he dealt with, she had balked at the idea of being fucked in the ass and had called him a pervert. Incensed by her refusal, he had beaten her unconscious, and then taken advantage of her when she was unable to fight back. He thought no more of the episode believing that she'd deserved the beating. She got back to her room, but was discovered unconscious the next morning and was rushed to hospital for emergency surgery to relieve the pressure from a blood clot on her brain. The hospital reported the incident to the police, and the madam of the establishment where the girl worked gave them Walsh's name, and he was arrested for first-degree assault and battery. Desperate, Walsh called his father to sort out the mess. His father reluctantly offered the madam of the brothel a large sum of money to withdraw her statement about the girl spending the previous night with Walsh, putting it down to a mix-up of clients. She couldn't identify the guilty person as he had given a false name. Later, the injured girl was also given a generous payment. Seán Walsh's protective mantle encouraged Simon to continue with his bad habits.

Unknown to Walsh, the girl herself never fully recovered from the beating. After regaining consciousness three days later, she was unable to remember anything of the events of that fateful night or even the name of her client. She continued to have blackouts for months after the incident and was eventually found dead in a backstreet alley, murdered in a petty mugging incident. She was hustled by two thieves, and blacked out while they dragged her into the alley. They stole her money and jewelry, and one decided to cut her throat for no apparent reason. Later, witnesses said they thought she was drunk, and was being helped by the two men.

This jam was no worse than the one in New Orleans, Walsh thought, but he overlooked the fact that his father was no longer around to help him. In fact, he considered the situation to be much better than the one in New Orleans because there were no witnesses and there would probably be no body and, therefore, no forensic evidence. The effect of the whiskey was beginning to cloud his thought processes, as he had drunk about a third of the bottle in the two glasses he'd had already. He poured himself another large glass, and in his light-headedness decided he would call his wife. He didn't enjoy the best of relations with her, and they hadn't spoken during his vacation, which was normal.

They led parallel lives, despite living and working together. In his inebriated state he believed that the sound of her voice would give him succor. He picked up the telephone, got an outside line, and dialed his home number in New York. Francesca the maid answered the phone and after exchanging the usual pleasantries passed it to his wife, Bridget.

"Hello, Simon!" said the voice at the other end of the line flatly. "I didn't expect to hear from you before the end of your vacation. Is everything alright with you?"

"I was a fool to think I'd get a warm welcome," he thought. "Yes, everything's fine. I just wanted to call to see how you were."

"That's unexpected, but there's really no need," Bridget replied dispassionately. "You should be out enjoying yourself

— sailing or whatever — while you can. I've got plenty to keep me occupied while you're away."

Walsh ignored the brush off and said, "I was out sailing today but wasn't feeling too well, so I only stayed out for a short time. I came back to the hotel and I've had a few stiff drinks to help me get to sleep." Walsh laughed at the thought of the disapproving face Bridget would now be making. In his drunken stupor, he thought Bridget could unknowingly give him an alibi if questioned later by police, in confirming he said he was only out in his boat for a short time.

"Well, as long as you're alright. Thanks for the call, Simon, but I must go now. Enjoy the last day of your vacation, and I'll see you when you get back."

Bridget put down the phone abruptly not waiting for her husband's reply. Walsh slammed the phone down onto the receiver, picturing Bridget's face in the black plastic, and staring at it contemptuously. Was it any wonder he behaved the way he did when she made him feel small and treated him like shit?

Staring into a mirror in his room, he noticed a red stain on his shirt. It wasn't a large stain but was unmistakably blood. He put his glass down on a coffee table, and started to rip off his shirt, not wanting the blood to come in contact with his skin. Half the buttons were torn off his Ralph Lauren casual shirt when he rolled it into a ball and hurled it into one corner of the room.

Walsh went back to the sofa and sat in the darkness of his hotel room. He decided that he was going to finish off the rest of the bottle of Jim Beam, then go out on the town and sleep with as many whores as he could. He was in no condition to do anything, particularly as far as having sex was concerned. By the time he'd had another large glass of whiskey, he was close to passing out. Before he drifted off into the kind of deep sleep that only large quantities of alcohol can induce, he satisfied himself in his own mind that he had nothing to worry about, and by the time morning came around, he wouldn't remember a thing.

Walsh didn't appreciate that it's virtually impossible to do anything without people noticing, especially a high-profile holidaymaker known to vacation frequently in Miami; one with a reputation for spending a lot of money. Most significantly, Walsh couldn't know that Jack Cates was planning to redress the balance by making him suffer for his treatment of Elsa. Jack had far more street savvy than Walsh, and was also a strong, determined man who usually got his way.

6:

FIX IT

"She'll be alright after a while; once the soreness in her shoulder has eased off," said Doc Brandt. "Make sure she sticks to her medication, and don't let her pamper herself, otherwise it will stiffen up. She'll be sore for a while, but no irreparable damage has been done. There'll be a faint scar where the bullet creased her, but a bit of makeup should cover it up, and it will fade with time." Jack had got in touch with Brandt, who lived in Florida, immediately after returning to his hotel, and was relieved that within an hour, the doctor had arrived to treat Elsa.

Doc Brandt was the man who did whatever was necessary to patch up knife or gunshot wounds or any other suspicious injury that would lead to awkward questions from hospital staff or the police. He was a qualified doctor who had been accused of carrying out backstreet abortions (before legalization), and was in serious danger of being dragged in front of the medical ethics committee. Contacts he had already nurtured with senior figures in organized crime syndicates in Florida used their influence to ensure that these allegations were not carried any further. One favor begets another and he now belonged to them, and became a well-known figure in the underworld. Jack knew him from his time with the NYPD when he was assigned to help the FBI with a drug-trafficking case. The Miami Police Department were also providing a support to the FBI through Gene Tanner, a detective with the MPD.

Brandt had aged since their last meeting, and Jack guessed he was in his late sixties. He remembered him as a tall man with a wiry build and angular features, who had the habit of perching his glasses on the top of his hooked nose, and looking over the top rim when talking to patients or their friends and relatives. He was now noticeably stooped and moved with arthritic stiffness, which would probably worsen as he got older, but like all medical professionals, he was slow to address the complaints of his own body.

Cocaine shipped from Columbia to Florida was being transferred to New York by road, and the outfit handling the transfer in Miami were given a cut for managing the merchandise. It was a smooth operation and the actual client, Mario Pallacio, was pleased at the way his Floridian colleagues were meeting their commitments. It was a tried and tested method of importing the drugs and all of the necessary palms had been greased to make sure nothing untoward would happen to the deliveries.

Unfortunately, one of their gang at the Miami end wanted more than the fee Mario was paying them, and decided to cream off some of the merchandise to sell locally. Of course, the shortfalls in the amounts delivered to New York became apparent, particularly as the quantities removed grew, as confidence in the lack of detection increased. Mario sent Leonard Tuzio down to Florida to sort out the situation, identify the thief and take the necessary action.

Around the same time, one of the trucks carrying a cocaine delivery to New York had been picked up on the outskirts of the city during a routine search following a traffic violation. The FBI were called in to handle the investigation, but came to rely heavily on the assistance provided by the two local policeman, who were aware of the people involved in drug trafficking in New York and Miami. The two men, working in similar capacities in their home towns and being fanatical about the NFL, became friends. Gene took Jack to a Miami Dolphins and New York Jets game, and was confident of a win with his team playing on home territory, but ended up paying Jack $100 on a side bet.

Inevitably, Tuzio pruned out the guilty party that was stealing from the cocaine deliveries, but was wounded in the resulting skirmish from a slice across his midriff by a switchblade. The FBI cleaned up the battle site, and weren't too concerned about gangsters killing each other, particularly now that the traffic route was known and couldn't be used in the future. They were unaware of Tuzio's involvement and happy about stopping the Miami end of the operation. Jack had recognized Tuzio from CCTV footage of arrivals at Miami airport, and Gene had kept tabs on him and knew the hotel where he was staying. He raided his hotel, hoping to get something that would tie his unwanted visitor to the cocaine shipments. Jack accompanied Gene as an observer, but all they found was Doc Brandt stitching up Tuzio's wound. Without any solid evidence to implicate Tuzio with the drug bust, they reluctantly allowed him to return to New York.

Later, Brandt's name was given to Gene by one of his snitches after a wounding in a homicide case. He had tried to use the doctor as a lead to the contract killer wounded by the police while escaping the scene of the crime. Nothing had come of the investigation, and the killer was never found, despite Gene's harassment of Brandt.

In more recent times, Jack had once again come into contact with the rogue doctor through his association with Roland Bannister. The wounding of one of his waiters at the Blue Cockatoo led to Bannister asking for medical services from Mario Pallacio, who relished the situation of being able to shower his benevolence on Roland. In Pallacio's world, one good turn always deserved another, and, therefore, his favor put Bannister further into his debt. He decided it would be better to use an outsider to avoid leaving a trail that could be traced. Once contact had been made with Brandt, Bannister was then able to access his services directly with Pallacio's approval. Jack made all the necessary arrangements to get Brandt to New York.

Jack was relieved at Brandt's confirmation that Elsa had only sustained a minor injury but was worried about how quickly the wound would heal. "Could the wound be infected?" he asked Brandt.

"Well, it's generally not a good idea to go swimming in the sea with a cut because the salt water is not sterile and can carry bacteria. This isn't such a problem down here, especially as she was bobbing on the top of the water, not going down to look at the reef. There is a nasty flesh-eating bacterium, but provided you keep the wound open, and clean it out with the medication I'm going to give you, she should be OK. If the wound starts to look sore and she feels sick, give me a call."

Brandt turned to Elsa and said, "Don't forget to leave it open for a couple of days and let it heal naturally."

The doctor never let Jack forget their earlier relationship when they were on opposite sides of the fence, particularly when asking for payment, which caused Jack the greatest discomfort. As Brandt walked toward him, Jack picked up the telephone and made a long-distance call to New York. Smiling Brandt held out his hand to receive his payment. Cradling the phone under his chin, Jack took out an envelope from the inside pocket of his jacket and handed it to the doctor, who in turn handed him the prescription for the medication for Elsa. "It's always good to do business with you, Jack," said Brandt, smirking and waving goodbye to Elsa before he left the room.

"Roland," Jack replied as a familiar voice came down the telephone line. "Listen. Elsa and I need a big favor."

"Favors cost money, Jack. You know that. I always pay you when you do something for me," said Bannister, who was used to the banter he was able to exercise with Jack and enjoyed the repartee. Although Jack worked for him from time to time, he was not entirely dependent on him for his income, as he also had his own interests such as his detective agency and the scams he ran with Elsa. They had been involved in a couple of deals together in the past when Jack had made the necessary introductions to useful contacts, but he was strictly the junior partner in these ventures, as Bannister had always put up the cash.

"Don't fuck with me, Roland! Elsa's been hurt on the Walsh job."

"If Elsa's been hurt on one of your cheap tricks, there'll be hell to pay," Bannister interjected.

"Calm down, Roland! She's taken a small gunshot wound in the shoulder. Fortunately, Doc Brandt was able to see her at short notice. He says Elsa will be OK as the wound is minor and she'll recover quickly." Jack knew that Bannister would be angry when he heard the news of Elsa's injury, not because she was his main attraction at the Blue Cockatoo, but because he carried a torch for her. He tried to conceal his feelings but the usual tell-tale signs were all evident whenever the two were together.

Jack knew he'd have to give all the details to Bannister to get his backing, explain how he and Elsa had become separated after the pickup, and run through the events that led to the shooting, toning down some of the grislier elements of Walsh's assault. When Bannister heard that Walsh had tried to rape Elsa, he started shouting at Jack again, threatening to hold him personally accountable for any psychological trauma that could affect her performances at the Blue Cockatoo.

"Can't you understand she has to be the ultimate sex object to every customer in the club? She can't do that if she's too frightened to get close to them," said Bannister.

"Listen, Roland," said Jack apologetically, trying to break the barrage of abuse being hurled at him. "How many millionaires or heads of wealthy business corporations do you know that are psychopathic? I had no idea the guy was going to freak out the way he did."

"OK. I know it's not really your fault, but you go too close to the line on these scams. It's not always possible to control a guy when he's got his pants around his ankles, because all he wants to do is cover up and break free. The real wonder is that no one's been injured before this. Elsa's special, you should know that, but you don't seem to appreciate her," said Bannister with rare sincerity.

The depth of emotion in Bannister's voice surprised Jack, who hadn't appreciated the full depth of the affection he had for Elsa.

"It won't happen again, Roland. You know I always plan these cons meticulously, but in this case, things just spiraled out of my control and ended up putting her at risk. But there can still be a payoff from this, one that could be big enough for all three of us."

Jack paused, waiting for Bannister either to explode again or consider the potential of making some ready money.

"If that's the case, the payoff has got to be very big," Bannister replied. "That bastard should be eager to pay us a lot of money if it's going to save his skin. The inmates are generally not very kind to men sent down for sex crimes or killing women. Someone of his delicate disposition would not like prison life at all, particularly if he found himself the victim of rape, instead of the perpetrator. Life's full of small ironies isn't it?"

"Don't get too carried away Roland. Your days as an attorney are long gone, but I'm glad you caught onto my train of thought so quickly. Walsh could find himself in a very vulnerable position if we can fabricate a strong case of murder against him; it will have to be based on circumstantial evidence, but may be sufficient for the police to take him to an arraignment hearing, even without a body."

"We need witnesses who saw Elsa and Walsh go out together and who can confirm he came back alone," Bannister replied.

"Yes, but we've got to move quickly before the trail goes cold! If I were in Walsh's position, I would want to get away from Miami as soon as possible, especially considering that Elsa's body could be washed onto the beach within a couple of days. Don't forget he probably believes that he's murdered her."

"We need to make a missing person's report to the police so they're aware of Elsa's disappearance. I'll send her roommate Julie down to look for Elsa and report her disappearance to the police," said Bannister, taking decisive action to move things forward.

"The police won't act on the strength of a missing person report from a friend unless it can be corroborated by someone at the marina, and I think I know just the man for the job, but it will cost money."

"What's new? I'll wire you $20,000, although you don't have to use it all if you can avoid it," Bannister suggested, and added, "Let's get the ball rolling as quickly as we can, I can already smell the money."

"You said yourself that we need witnesses who can confirm the movements of Walsh and Elsa at the marina. I'll give you a ring when the pieces are in place, and the police have sufficient concern about the reason behind Elsa's disappearance to chase Walsh." Jack replaced the phone on the cradle, and went in the bedroom to check on Elsa.

In the half-light of the early morning, he could see her lying on the bed with the sheets pulled up to her chin and her knees circling up to her body. She still looked beautiful. She turned her head slowly and beckoned Jack to the bed. Jack sat down on the edge of the bed and lay down beside her. Elsa shifted her position to face him, closing her eyes as he bent down to kiss her softly on the lips.

"I can't do this anymore," Elsa whispered. "I really thought I was going to die out there."

She paused for a second and shuddered at the thought of what might have happened. Jack gently took her in his arms and whispered how guilty he felt about the whole thing. It was enough that he had told her, and she cuddled up closer to him.

Jack was never going to put her in such a position again, but he would have to tell her he was planning one last big job that would set them both up for life. He knew it sounded like the same old record, but this time, she wouldn't have to be working at the sharp end, and would also make Walsh suffer for what he had done to her. A sudden feeling of guilt washed over him for the times he had made her play the whore to compromise all of those rich, unfeeling bastards that they had ripped off in the past. Roland's words about him not appreciating her echoed in his ears.

Mention of yet another sting broke Elsa's feeling of warmth in Jack's arms.

"I have to flaunt my body in front of those sad bastards in the Blue Cockatoo," Elsa cried, "but I don't have to let anybody touch me anymore." Her voice faded as if she was making a pact with herself.

She was still shaken eight hours after falling into the water, and was now reappraising her life. With Jack, there would always be one more score no matter how big the pay off. They had made a lot of money together from this racket, and up to now, it had been fairly easy with most of the marks being too embarrassed to make a fuss or afraid of their wives finding out about their philandering. She had been carefully saving her half of the money while Jack had spent it on lavish gifts to her or his family, or lost it with gambling and reckless spending, or had simply given it away. He was a man that would always need more money.

"Listen, Elsa," Jack pleaded. "You won't have to put up with this kind of life any more. Walsh thinks you're dead and that he murdered you. We have got to get some other people to think the same thing; to convince the world you're dead. But that means you've got to disappear." Jack paused to let Elsa fully take in what he was saying.

"But I thought that you were going to make him suffer for what he did to me. I thought you were going to hurt the bastard," Elsa shouted. "He tried to rape me, for God's sake! Don't you care about that?"

"Of course, I care Elsa, but we've got to be calm, think logically, and be smart! There's only a short-term benefit in the satisfaction of me beating him up, which I could easily do. But we would be no better off after it, and you would have nothing to show for the hell you've been through. If my plan succeeds, we'll be able to get a small fortune out of him that will get us out of this fucking rat race and let us start over somewhere else on our own terms."

Jack stared intensely at Elsa, willing her to understand the wisdom in what he was suggesting. Elsa looked back at Jack, searching for a sign that she meant more to him than the money he was expecting to squeeze out of Walsh. The emotion drained from her face when she saw that the excitement of working another angle — another scam — was greater than the anger he felt over what Walsh had done to her.

"OK, Jack," she said resignedly, "but after that, things will have to change."

Elsa might have reconsidered her decision had she known what lay ahead of her.

7:

MISSING

Julie's plane landed in Miami at 6:00 in the evening, and she booked into the same hotel as Elsa. Jack had booked her into a separate hotel to ensure that he and Julie could not be linked in case Walsh or the police made any enquiries about the hotel Elsa stayed in. After settling into her room, Julie made discreet enquiries about her friend's whereabouts and was informed she had not been seen there since the previous morning. The clerk advised her that Elsa should have checked out earlier — before 12:00 — and that they were storing her belongings so that they could prepare the room for the next guest. He added that they would keep Elsa's belongings until her bill was settled.

Julie then went to Jack's hotel and found his room number from one of the receptionists. She knocked on the door, and was greeted by Jack's smiling face. Instead of returning his smile, Julie pushed past him and went straight into the apartment to find Elsa sitting on the sofa in pajamas Jack had bought for her earlier. Julie rushed over to hug her.

"Gently," Elsa complained, "I'm still sore."

"I guess this is all thanks to lover boy over there," Julie replied, "who doesn't seem to mind putting your ass on the line."

Of course, Jack had once been Julie's 'lover boy'.

"Take it easy, Julie. Jack couldn't have known the way Walsh would behave when I was alone with him on his boat. We got separated, so he couldn't step in at the right moment, as he normally does. I feel equally responsible, because I shouldn't have gone out on Walsh's boat. The risks were obvious, and I was too complacent."

"It could have turned out worse," Jack interjected, "but it didn't and now we've got to make this trip to Miami worthwhile. Roland, Elsa and I have a plan to put Walsh on the spot, and we want you to help us. We'll make it worth your while."

Julie turned from Jack to Elsa who nodded to confirm what he was saying and that Roland supported them. "This means that I've got to disappear to make it look as if Walsh really did kill me and make others suspicious about my not returning with him to the marina," Elsa added.

"I understand," Julie replied, even though she was at a loss to understand why Elsa was meekly continuing to do just as Jack wanted. After a short pause, she added, "Roland told me to talk to you and Jack, and follow your instructions."

"I want you to go to the police tomorrow and report Elsa missing. Tell them you've not heard from her in two days and that she was supposed to ring you before leaving Miami to arrange a pickup at the airport," said Jack.

"But tomorrow's Sunday. Why would I wait to call the police?"

"When Elsa didn't ring on Friday night you became concerned, particularly when you had no word by Saturday morning. You didn't want to ring alarm bells if it wasn't necessary, knowing that sometimes she'd lose track of time if she was enjoying herself, so you arranged a flight to Miami to check things out."

"Doesn't that seem a bit extreme?" Julie asked.

"Normally, I would say 'Yes', but in this instance, it was important for Elsa to confirm her flight with you because she had made an appointment with her stockbroker, before leaving for Miami, to discuss her investments. That bit is actually true and provides a good reason for you to be concerned as she was adamant about keeping the appointment before her body clock changed to suit her working hours at the Blue Cockatoo. What time did you arrive in Miami?"

"About 6:00," Julie replied.

"Good. That fits in with the general framework of the story. In the meantime, I'll grease some wheels down at the marina," said Jack.

"What do I do after going to the cops? It would be a shame not to make the most of this trip while I'm here."

Neither Jack nor Elsa were surprised at Julie's response, knowing her own welfare was always top of her list. Jack gave Julie $1,000 to cover the flight ticket and other expenses while she was in Miami. What he didn't know was that Bannister had bought her flight ticket and also given her $1,000 for expenses. Julie smiled, thinking that she would have plenty of time for shopping before returning to New York.

After talking to Julie, Jack drove over to the marina and waited for the motorboat attendant to collect his car after work. He spotted the man entering the car park and got out to intercept him before he reached it, putting his hand on the man's shoulder as he went to open the car door. The man turned anxiously, not knowing what to expect, but relaxed when he recognized Jack's face.

"Hi!" said Jack. "How's the motorboat business?"

"It don't matter to me. I don't own the fucking business," the man replied in a matter-of-fact way, shrugging his shoulders to emphasize the point.

"You know everyone who works at the marina, though, don't you?"

"Well, I've been working there for the last ten years, so I oughta," the man replied with growing interest.

"Simon Walsh took his boat out yesterday afternoon with a very pretty young woman aboard. Trouble was I heard that he came back alone," said Jack as the man looked back at him impassively. "It must be a long swim back to the marina from wherever they went in his boat, and my guess is that she didn't make it."

"Could be, but what's that got to do with me?"

Jack paused to study the attendant for a moment. He was a typical middle-aged underachiever with few interests outside his job other than perhaps sport or DIY. After work, he would usually have a quick drink at his local bar where he would tell anyone who cared to listen what was wrong with the world, and what needed to be done to put it right. He probably felt he was underprivileged, but through no fault of his own as he never had the breaks other people got to make a success of his life. Despite his aggressive demeanor, Jack sensed that he would be amenable and useful, given the right incentive.

"If anything's happened to that girl it would be a shame, but it could also affect the people working at the marina. If the cops or health and safety are called in, God knows what can of worms would be opened. It would be better if the authorities are advised, rather than finding out by accident. If she's dead, her body could get washed up on the shore, or the police might get the statement of a witness to what happened while they were out at sea."

"If you're so worried, why don't you go to the cops?"

"I could, but I wasn't involved or a witness to what led to her getting on Walsh's boat, so I don't have anything worthwhile to tell them. On the other hand, you must know others at the marina who can give the police a steer on what happened."

"If I get involved with the police, what am I gonna say? I didn't see her get on Walsh's boat. I'm just taking your word for it, and listening to some of the talk I've heard around the marina. Besides, Walsh is an influential man, and I value my crummy job, 'cause it's all I got!"

"You don't have to put your neck on the line. We both have the same dilemma, knowing something happened but not able to do anything about it. The difference between us is that you know some of the people who would make good witnesses."

"Who?" the perplexed attendant asked.

"Walsh picked her up at the Drop Inn, so the barman must have seen them leaving together, and somebody told me he had just had the boat refueled. His maintenance guy would also have seen her."

"Why are you so anxious to get him clipped?"

"To tell you the truth, I don't like Walsh or the reputation he has for the way he treats women, and I want to see him get what's coming to him," Jack answered, and added, "What's your name?" trying to put the conversation on a more personal footing.

"Al, if it's anything to do with you."

"Like I said, Al, you don't have to go to the authorities yourself. I want you to raise doubts in those other guy's minds. Between them, they probably have sufficient information to give the cops a complete picture. I just want you to make them understand what has happened and the importance of their coming forward."

"That's easier said than done," Al replied.

"Like I said, there's something in it for you. Here's $5,000," said Jack, handing him an envelope. "If you and your work colleagues find it necessary to report their concerns to the police, you'll receive another envelope with the same amount of money in it. If not, I'll be back to collect this," he said, pointing at the envelope he had just handed over.

"That's a big incentive," said Al, looking inside the envelope before putting it into his jacket pocket. "Have the money ready, the job's as good as done."

With that, he climbed into his car, and drove off.

Sunday morning was a nice, warm, clear day with a light breeze. At 8:00, Al was talking to the mechanic, Joe Weaver, who had serviced and refueled Walsh's boat.

"Say, Joe, that was a fine piece of ass that Walsh went out on his boat with on Friday, the lucky bastard. It just shows what money can get you, don't it?"

"Yeah, while I'm up to my neck in grease, he's out at sea relaxing with a beautiful broad. Where's the justice? Everything he's got was built by his old man; he hasn't earned a penny of it."

"Have you seen that broad before? She's sure hard to forget," Al pressed.

"No, I haven't," the mechanic replied. "And I've not seen her since. Walsh hasn't been out on his boat since Friday. We won't get the chance of seeing her again, because I think he's leaving today."

"That's a pity. I was hoping to get another look at her before Walsh finished his vacation. I bet she looked a little more ruffled getting off the boat than she did getting on it! As I said, what a lucky bastard that guy is!"

"Come to think of it, I didn't see her getting off the boat," said Joe, scratching his head. Walsh got back at about 6:30, and insisted I clean the boat before finishing because he wasn't going out again and wanted it mothballed for next year. I couldn't see the urgency and left it. I'll do it when I get around to it."

"But you said the broad wasn't on the boat. That seems strange, doesn't it?" said Al, trying to keep the mechanic's thoughts focused in the right direction.

"Walsh called me over to the boat as soon as he moored. I definitely would have seen her getting off the boat if she'd been aboard. I don't know why she wasn't with him," he said as much to himself as to Al. "She couldn't have been on board. It never struck me as strange at the time. I was more interested in tidying up and getting home."

"There must be a logical reason for it. He must have dropped her off elsewhere," Al replied.

He knew the mechanic would realize that her disembarking elsewhere was not a likely proposition as they had only been out for about three hours and there were no free berths within a traveling distance of one and a half hours. The seed of doubt had been planted in Joe Weaver's mind and that was enough.

Mid-morning, Al went into the Ocean Drop Inn, and repeated his patter about the stunning woman with Walsh on Friday afternoon.

"I don't know if she was a hooker or not," said Jerry. "She certainly didn't look like the kind of hooker you'd see downtown, but she latched onto Walsh as soon as he came into the bar. He's always had a roving eye, so he would probably have made a beeline for her, even if the place had been packed."

"I only saw her from a distance, but she didn't look like no hooker to me either," said Al.

"I know what you mean. With looks like hers, she wouldn't need to ply her trade on the streets; she'd be into a much higher class of clientele. Sure, she was a looker, but she was sophisticated too, you know, in the way she handled herself and moved. There was nothing cheap about her, but I guess she could have been searching for a high roller like Simon Walsh. Whatever the reason, they left here with his hand on her ass."

"They may have left together, but it don't seem they came back together," Al replied.

He went on to recount his conversation with the mechanic. Al was satisfied after talking to Jerry that he had introduced sufficient doubt in his mind to prick his conscience about the young woman's safety and he knew his concern would grow the more he thought about it. Al was confident that both Jerry and the mechanic would go to the police to report their suspicion of foul play on Walsh's boat. Police enquiries would subsequently lead to corroboration of their stories, and kick off an investigation into Elsa's whereabouts after she met Walsh in the Ocean Drop Inn.

Julie walked into the 10th Precinct Station to report Elsa missing at the same time as Al was talking to Jerry. She strode to the front desk and asked for the duty sergeant, and made a statement on Elsa's disappearance as Jack had instructed her. Although the sergeant took her statement with a resigned air that said he had heard her story many times before, his attitude would change later when three witnesses from the marina were brought into the station to make formal statements about a missing person.

A police officer had been sent to the marina on Monday afternoon following a telephone call from Joe the mechanic to the police station. Interviews included sessions with Joe, Jerry and Al, although Al kept a low profile by ensuring his testimony was based on the conversations he had with the other two and would not be admissible as evidence. He did confirm, however, that he had seen Walsh and Elsa together at the marina as they walked across the wharf to Walsh's boat.

After taking formal statements the police felt they had sufficient justification to question Walsh, who had left Miami on Sunday and was now at home in New York. They told Joe not to touch or go on the boat, but to leave it exactly as it was. Detective Tanner rang Walsh on Monday evening to request an interview with him on the following Wednesday. They agreed a time of 2:30 in the afternoon, when Walsh knew his wife would be out.

8:

HOME

Walsh quickly replaced the receiver of the phone when he heard his wife coming into the hallway.

"Francesca says dinner will be ready in 30 minutes, Simon; that should give you plenty of time to freshen up and dress ahead of the concert this evening. It's scheduled to start at 8:00, and I don't want to arrive late." Bridget Walsh gave her husband a disdainful look as he smiled and bowed subserviently in acceptance of her instructions. "You can put your business matters on hold for one evening in the year, and at least, give me a little support, as I am the president of the charity that will benefit from the money made by the concert. Oh, just please hurry up."

Smiling thinly at Bridget, Walsh watched her as she ascended the stairs without a backward glance toward him. She had spoken and clearly expected him to obey. He followed her up the stairs and went into his bedroom. He poured himself a glass of whiskey and loosened his tie. Tanner had not been specific about the purpose of his visit, and that led Walsh to wonder if it was connected to Lisa Millarno. Tanner had told Walsh he was following a routine line of enquiry concerning an incident at the marina where his boat was berthed and that he might be able to assist him. Although he felt a little agitated after the call, Walsh decided that he would wait until he heard what Tanner had to say before starting to worry about being implicated in any crime.

Bridget sat at her dressing table, and picked up the VIP guest list for their evening's event. She looked into the mirror, and brushed a wisp of blond hair away from her forehead. She was an elegant woman who moved in a natural and unaffected way. Her blond hair and pale complexion betrayed her North European ancestry. Her figure was slight, even willowy, giving the impression of a delicate frame; the inner strength she needed to remain in control of her loveless marriage with Simon Walsh was, however, a measure of her strong determination and fighting spirit.

Being the great granddaughter of a Polish immigrant, who, after arriving in the United States at the end of the First World War, had built up a company doing steel fabrication and erection, resilience was part of her genetic makeup. Her great grandfather began working as a site laborer, rapidly progressed to foreman and then construction manager. It was only a matter of time before he branched out on his own, initially with small contracts, but he inevitably built his company into a well-respected and trusted concern with a reputation for delivering work on time and to a high standard. Her father, Pawel Koslowski, who, like his grandfather had started work at the basement level after getting an engineering degree, had worked very hard to become chief executive. He took great pride in the reputation of the company for competitiveness with quality and in his own good name.

The collapse of a partially-built steel frame during the construction of an office block, resulted in the death of one of the steelwork erectors, and there was a threat of legal action for negligence arising from use of sub-standard materials. The public inquiry into the incident had uncovered false certificates issued with the imported steel, and found that the original overseas steelwork supplier had disappeared following a number of similar complaints over the poor quality of their steel products. After the findings of the inquiry were released, confidence in Koslowski and his company had evaporated and their order book was empty. Koslowski's only real mistake had been in not verifying the credentials of the supplier before signing contracts. They had been the only firm able to deliver the steel in the very short timescales required by the construction contract. Within a few months following the accident, all of Koslowski's workforce had been laid off, and many had found new employment elsewhere. His business was now reduced to a hollow shell. Despite this setback, Koslowski was convinced he would eventually be exonerated and that business would get back on its feet.

Bridget's father already suffered from poor health and this incident visibly aged him, highlighting his frailties, and he had lost confidence in his own judgement and ability to manage the business. Bridget was concerned that further pressure would result in irrevocable deterioration of his health, and could even be life threatening because of his heart condition. She found it hard to reconcile the frail body and spirit of her father with the strong giant of a man that she worshipped in her childhood. She was a qualified accountant and was part of the family business, working as the company secretary. In dealing with the loss adjuster of the National Mutual Provident over the company's insurance claim, she met Simon Walsh, their financial director, son of the chief executive, Seán.

When Bridget greeted Simon on his first visit to their offices, she was pleased to find that he was considerate and sensitive to her company's present circumstances and the poor health of her father. He explained at great length that his involvement in the case was driven by the need to expedite the claim quickly and because her father was a loyal and valued customer. The day went well and Walsh asked her to have dinner with him that evening. Although her initial reaction was not to accept the invitation, she agreed to dine with Walsh, hoping that a friendly working relationship between them might help promote a benevolent approach in his administration of the claim.

Walsh took her to the most expensive restaurant in town and spent the whole evening talking about himself, his father and his important role in the running of the National Mutual Provident. He clearly enjoyed Bridget's company and his single purpose during the whole of the evening appeared to be the need to impress her.

The couple dined together on several occasions during the course of Walsh's investigation into the insurance claim, and she quickly became bored with his preoccupation with himself. By this time, she had learned he planned to take over the running of the National Mutual Provident when his father retired and had lofty ambitions to enter politics, and eventually run for Congress. The more time she spent with him, the more she began to see through the shallow veneer of his public face and recognized that he was ruthlessly ambitious and egocentric. The full depth of his ruthlessness only surfaced during their last dinner date.

"Your father's in a tight spot," said Walsh while he was ordering the after-dinner liquors. "He should have arranged for independent testing of the steel by an accredited test house. It's good practice when importing steel, and it's also a condition of the insurance agreement. Your father can't hack it anymore and now he's going to lose the company. He could even end up going to prison."

Walsh's sudden change of attitude unsettled Bridget and she fought her natural desire to retaliate. "We don't normally carry out independent tests, unless specifically requested by the client," she replied. "The company who supplied the steel sent us evidence of testing on previous contracts and we checked the company was an accredited supplier in their own country and internationally. We also checked that they used suitable test houses, locally available to the production plant, to test the steel."

Unfazed by Bridget's interjection, Walsh continued, "You may not be aware of this requirement because you're only a small company and don't normally import your steel. The steel for the other contracts you've undertaken in the past was sourced within the United States. I know the tight lead-in to delivery forced your father to go elsewhere, but he was negligent in the execution of his responsibilities and did not comply with the requirements of the insurance policy. If I report these facts, the insurance claim will not be paid and your father could be prosecuted for criminal negligence."

Bridget began to feel nauseous at the thought of her father going to prison, afraid of the detrimental effect imprisonment would have on him, as he prized his good reputation more than money. Unable to find an argument that would mitigate her father's failure to carry out independent tests, she pleaded to Walsh's better nature.

"My father's been with your company for 20 years without a single claim. Surely, that must count for something." She couldn't believe what she was saying, but was now desperate.

"Not as far as my company's shareholders are concerned," Walsh replied pompously. "But I'm sure that if I'm frugal with the actual details in my report, something can be done about your claim," he continued as he covered Bridget's hand with his. Walsh felt her hand stiffen on his touch and he began to squeeze it more tightly until she couldn't move it, or break free. "I've enjoyed our time together, Bridget, and I'd like to think we've grown close to each other. My initial objective was simply to fuck you, but now I think you can be of much greater use to me."

The crudeness of Walsh's last statement made her cringe, but despite her discomfort, Bridget's only concern was for her father, so she accepted his overfamiliarity and rough handling without complaint. She relaxed and his grip on her hand eased. "My father is due to retire; in fact, it would be unwise for him to continue running the firm in his current state of health. He would be satisfied if his current financial commitments were honored by the claim and the matter of the independent test certificates was not taken any further," said Bridget.

"That's asking a lot," Walsh replied. "My father is also due to retire soon and keeps telling me that it's good business practice to have a wife around when running a company. You're both attractive and intelligent, and have a solid commercial nous from working with your father. I wouldn't expect you to work directly for my company as you do for your father, but you know how business is conducted and that would be useful when entertaining associates and clients."

"Yes, but how does that help my father?" Bridget asked coldly.

"I will suddenly find correspondence from your father to an independent test house requesting sample testing of the steel. I will also find test certificates from the independent test house that verify the quality of the steel. These documents will demonstrate your father complied with the requirements of the insurance policy. Test certificates from verification tests undertaken by my company will corroborate the findings of the independent test house. The accident will, therefore, be put down to poor workmanship and your father's reputation will remain unblemished," said Walsh confidently. "It's a tall order but there are several people who owe me favors, which I can 'cash in' to settle this business."

"That will undermine the insurance claim of the victim's family," Bridget replied.

She felt compromised over protecting her father at the expense of others, but knew deep down she had no real alternative.

"Someone has got to lose out, I'm sure you wouldn't like it to be your father. This way he can retire with a bit of money in his pocket," Walsh replied with a smug grin.

Bridget nodded in agreement, her eyes fixed on the table, not wishing to give Walsh the pleasure of seeing her inner torment.

"Good! Now let's get things off to a good start," Walsh continued.

He called the waiter, paid the bill and took Bridget to his hotel and they consummated their agreement. Walsh used Bridget's body as an object for his own gratification without any consideration of her needs or sensitivities. His discovery that she was a virgin heightened the level of his excitement. In the morning, they agreed a schedule for the coming months that would ultimately lead to their marriage.

On her return home, Bridget explained to her father that the insurance claim had been settled, and convinced him that he should now retire rather than risk further deterioration to his health. She also told him that she would be marrying Simon Walsh and moving to New York in the near future. Her father lived long enough to see her marry Walsh, but died shortly after that, blaming himself for the loss of his father's company and not providing for his workforce.

Walsh and Bridget went on honeymoon to Niagara Falls. After dining together, they went to their hotel room. She had endured months of sleeping with an inconsiderate lover and decided to draw a halt to her abuse on their wedding night. They got into bed and Walsh began groping her in the manner that had become normal. As he buried his head in her breasts, she grabbed the hair on the back of his head and pulled it backward sharply.

"Now that we're married, don't think that I'm going to submit to your crude pawing and groping and pathetic excuse for lovemaking."

"But we're married now. You've got to!" Walsh replied, pulling his head free. "I'll make you if I have to!" he shouted threateningly.

"You rape me once more and I'll kill you in your sleep," said Bridget with a coldness that made Walsh shiver.

"If that's how you feel, why did you marry me after the insurance claim was settled?"

"You took a lot from me," Bridget answered. "Now it's my turn to get something in return. I'll be a good little wife in front of family, friends and business colleagues, but don't expect any more than that. And I also want to be involved in the running of the NMP, rather than being a token figure. I'm a chartered accountant and intend to keep on working."

They returned to New York the next day, and Walsh moved into a separate bedroom, explaining to Francesca, their maid, that he could only sleep properly when alone in his bed. Bridget took over as financial director at the NMP, and when at home or at work, her personal dealings with Walsh were restricted to business or domestic issues.

9:

QUIZ WALSH

Detective Tanner was prompt. Francesca greeted him at the front door of the luxury apartment and took him into the study for his meeting with Walsh. Tanner introduced himself, produced his police badge to confirm his identity and the two men shook hands. Walsh invited Tanner to take a seat and asked him if he would like a drink. In response, Tanner shook his head refusing the drink, and made himself comfortable in the chair facing Walsh, who then told the maid to leave the room.

The policeman was impressed by the size of the apartment and its luxuriant decor and fittings, which gave witness to the wealth of its residents. The carpets were all of pure wool, and the walls in the reception and corridor to Walsh's study were covered with wood paneling. In Walsh's study, the decor changed, the majority of the wall areas being covered by bookshelves and the remainder being dressed either in patterned leather or light wood panels, giving a very masculine feel to the room. The furniture was of heavy oak with the backrests and seats of the chairs clad with dark, studded, leather cushions.

Tanner, being used to the warmth of Florida, was wearing a coat to keep out the New York chill. His appearance was not the same as that of the local cops; he was more conventionally dressed in a dark-blue suit, white shirt and blue tie under his gabardine coat, which was belted at the waist. He was a big man, and appeared to have an athletic build.

"This is a very nice apartment you have here. I don't think I've seen anything quite like it in Miami," said Tanner, opening his coat to make himself more comfortable.

"You've come a long way to talk to me, Detective. There must be a better reason than seeing my apartment." As he spoke, Walsh poured himself a shot of Jim Beam, saying, "I know it's a little early in the day for this, but I'm not going back to work this afternoon, so what the hell! Are you sure you don't want to join me?"

"No, thank you, sir. There's nothing wrong with having a drink in the afternoon, but I'm on duty."

"But you can relax, can't you? You're more than a little out of your jurisdiction, so who's gonna tell?"

Tanner put his hands up, declining the offer.

"Well, what about a soda?" Walsh continued

"No, thank you. This isn't a social call; I'm collecting evidence for a case I'm working on. I have no authority here, but I must warn you that anything you say may be used as evidence, if it's relevant to my case. That also goes for evidence obtained through information you give me in our discussions. You can refuse to answer my questions if you wish."

"Clever bastard!" Walsh thought. "He knows with that statement he's made it difficult for me to kick him out. Besides, I need to know what he's come to see me about.

"I've got nothing to hide. I assume you want to talk to me about my recent vacation in Miami."

"Yes, I do. I'm investigating the disappearance of a young woman called Elsa Bartelli. Do you know her?"

Walsh had been expecting to hear Lisa Millarno's name and was relieved and pleasantly surprised at the name given to him.

"The name doesn't sound familiar. I really can't remember," he stammered. "I'm sure I would remember her name if we'd met."

"She's not the kind of woman that you would easily forget. Take a look at this picture I have of her," said Tanner, handing

Walsh a photograph. It was a publicity still from the Blue Cockatoo, which showed Elsa, in an exotic outfit, posing on stage.

Looking at the photograph, Walsh immediately recognized the woman in the picture, which made his stomach turn over. His earlier relief was replaced by anxiety, as he tried not to display any sign of fear that would be picked up by Tanner. An inner anger raged within him at his own stupidity in not anticipating that Lisa Millarno was a false name.

Finally, he said, "I see what you mean, Detective. She's certainly a stunner, but unfortunately I can't place her."

"That's strange," the policeman replied. "You were seen in conversation with her at the Ocean Drop Inn in Miami last Friday afternoon, and later, you both went out for a cruise in the boat you have berthed at the marina where the bar's located."

Tanner delivered his statement in a matter-of-fact way that was not intended to antagonize Walsh, but nevertheless irritated him because it exposed his lie. It was a stupid mistake, Walsh thought, as his liaison with Elsa could be easily checked and verified.

"Why have you been investigating my movements last Friday? Am I suspected of anything?"

"We don't know that any crime has been committed, Mr. Walsh. Miss Bartelli was seen drinking with you, and later, going out with you on your boat, but she hasn't been seen since and was reported missing on Sunday. Two independent witnesses confirm you were with her on Friday, both in the Ocean Drop Inn and on your boat."

"You have it all wrapped up, don't you, Detective? Your superiors will be impressed," Walsh replied, stalling for time while trying to collect his thoughts. His mind was racing beyond control and he was finding it difficult to string the simplest of sentences together.

Clutching at straws, he asked, "How is Commissioner Connor, by the way? I haven't seen him for some time."

"He retired last month, sir, and I believe he's enjoying his retirement in Palm Springs. Thanks for your interest, but can we return to my investigation? I have to catch a plane back to Miami at 5:30."

Walsh was getting more and more annoyed with the situation, particularly as he couldn't even use Connor as a threat to rattle Tanner. The face of the detective was impassive, devoid of expression or emotion, and didn't betray any doubts or misgivings he may have harbored about the man he was interviewing. Walsh decided to try and treat him as a friend by taking him into his confidence, hoping Tanner could empathize with his situation.

He took a gulp of his drink and said, "OK. I do know the woman. She called herself Lisa Millarno, and said she was in Miami visiting her sister. I went into the Ocean Drop Inn for a quick drink. She was sitting at the bar and came on to me. We went out for a short boat ride, but I found out she was just a tease, so I came straight back and that's the last I saw of her."

"Why did you lie when I first asked you if you knew her? How can I believe you're telling the truth now? I want you to answer my questions honestly, because if she's not found, we will have to delve deeper into her movements last Friday."

"Look. I'm a married man and I love my wife. I may party with other women while I'm away by myself, but I'm only human. My picking her up last Friday was like a hundred others I've had. They mean nothing and are quickly forgotten after my vacation. I was afraid of my wife finding out. That's why I lied!"

"That's all very well, Mr. Walsh, but it doesn't get me any nearer to finding out what has happened to Miss Bartelli, and your lying could indicate that you're implicated in her disappearance somehow."

Walsh couldn't contain himself any longer and shouted at Tanner, "What the hell are you trying to say? I've just fucking told you my reason for lying. That's the beginning and end of it! Do you understand?"

Tanner remained calm in the face of Walsh's aggression, saying, "I'm not trying to say anything — that's not my job. I only deal in facts and hard evidence. Miss Bartelli has been missing since last Friday, and you, Mr. Walsh, were the last person seen with her before her disappearance. The longer it takes us to establish her whereabouts, or for her to contact friends or relatives, the more suspicious the circumstances of her disappearance become. There's no obvious reason why she would wish to disappear. I'm sure you can understand that."

Tanner paused to take a breath and let the logic of his reasoning sink in with Walsh, whose anger had subsided, and he was now staring into his drink, either looking for inspiration or a place to hide. He couldn't bluster his way through this situation and he didn't have the guile to outwit Tanner.

The policeman continued, "Her roommate in New York had been expecting a call on Friday evening for a pickup at JFK the following day. She never got the call from Elsa and was unable to contact her at her hotel. Worried, she flew down to Miami on Saturday afternoon to find out if she was OK. There was no trace of Elsa at the hotel, and the hotel staff had not seen her since Friday morning."

"A couple of days isn't a long time to be incommunicado. She's a grown woman, for God's sake! She might have decided to extend her vacation, or gone off with some other sucker," Walsh reasoned.

"If she had done either of those things, her first thought would have been to cancel her return flight at the very least; nor did she check out of her hotel or pick up her luggage," Tanner replied. "You said she came onto you in the Ocean Drop Inn. How did she do that?" he asked, trying to understand the circumstances of their meeting and the banter between them that had led to her being invited onto Walsh's boat.

"Well, it's not too easy to explain. She didn't say or do anything, but had an air about her that said she was game for anything. After all, she came out with me on my boat minutes after first meeting me."

"Are you saying she was a prostitute?"

"No, of course not. It's just that she was friendlier than you would normally expect after just meeting a stranger. I'm used to girls making a pass at me because I'm rich and well connected, so I recognized the signs. They want to be given a good time and have money splashed out on them."

"You have had experience with prostitutes before, though, haven't you, Mr. Walsh?" Tanner interjected.

Walsh was startled by the switch in the line of questioning from Elsa to him and by the faint hint of antagonism in the tone of the policeman's voice. "Yes, I've been with prostitutes, if that's what you mean. I do a lot of traveling and sometimes need a little more than just company from the women I meet."

"Did you want 'more than just company' from Elsa, Mr. Walsh?" Tanner cut in.

"I told you she came onto me at the Ocean Drop Inn, so I naturally assumed she wanted us to spend some time together before her dinner date with her sister. It turned out that she was just being a tease, so we came straight back."

"Do you mean she wasn't prepared to have sex with you?"

"Yes, that's exactly what I mean," said Walsh, once again beginning to show the strain of the questioning on his face. "It soon became clear to me that she wanted money for sex, so it was pointless carrying on."

"But you've been with prostitutes before. Why was this any different? Why didn't you offer her money?"

"She didn't look like any hooker I've been with, and I thought she was being friendly because she liked me. I was looking for a little more than sex. I also wanted some friendly and witty company after what had been a boring day."

"But sometimes your sexual advances get out of hand, don't they? Rita Alonso is evidence of that," said Tanner, increasing the pressure on Walsh.

"Who the hell is Rita Alonso?" Walsh asked.

"She's the prostitute in New Orleans you very nearly beat to death."

"Oh, yes. I remember her now," Walsh replied weakly. "I caught her trying to steal my wallet after I'd already paid her very well. The incident blew up out of proportion for a short time, but in the end, she dropped the charges."

"Yes. Thanks to your father, she dropped the charges. You may have made her pay for her mistake, but to my mind, the severity of the punishment you meted out doesn't appear to have matched the crime. Is that what happened to Elsa?"

"No, it is not! If you are going to charge me with anything, I want to call my lawyer," said Walsh. "I've tried to give you honest answers but you're just twisting everything I say."

"I'm just trying to get to the truth, Mr. Walsh, and as I've said, I don't have the authority to charge you with anything. I have to ask these questions to ensure all avenues are covered in my investigation," Tanner replied in an attempt to calm Walsh so that he could carry on with his interview.

"I took Lisa or Elsa onto the boat, but when it became clear she was just after money, we had a couple of drinks and went back to the marina," said Walsh, having regained his composure.

"What time did you get back to the marina, Mr. Walsh?"

"I can't remember," Walsh blustered.

"Nobody can support your statement or remember you returning to the marina with Miss Bartelli. In fact, your mechanic, Joseph Weaver, says that you came back alone."

"He's mistaken. He can't be relied on to put enough fuel in the boat when I go out to sea, so he certainly can't be relied on to observe all of my comings and goings."

"That may be the case, but he seems certain about the fact you returned alone and the time you arrived back at the marina," Tanner replied without giving Walsh the time given in the mechanic's statement.

"In that case, it's a question of which of us you want to believe," Walsh retorted.

"Well, I can see you're upset and probably not in a frame of mind to answer my questions objectively, so let's finish. Thanks for your time," said Tanner, rising from his chair. "Oh, I forgot to mention your telephone call to your wife last Friday. The telephone records show that you called your wife early in the evening, so I'll need to talk to her to confirm the time of your conversation and what you said."

"Does that mean you're going to tell her about Lisa, I mean Elsa?" said Walsh through gritted teeth. He was seething underneath what appeared to be a calm exterior at the way Tanner had manipulated the interview and at how easily the detective was able to undermine the information Walsh had given him. Certain that Tanner would now take the matter further, Walsh added, "I'm sure the records show that we only talked for a couple of minutes; hardly enough time for me to tell her that I had met a beautiful woman and murdered her on my boat!"

"I need to confirm the timing of your movements on that day so that we can build an overall picture of events as they occurred. If you've nothing to hide, my investigation should help show you are innocent, and that is to your benefit."

"Very delicately put, but if you suspect me of murder, why didn't you come straight out with it rather than pussyfooting around?"

"I haven't mentioned murder," Tanner replied, "I haven't got all of the relevant information to come to any conclusion about the cause of her disappearance, and I certainly haven't put you down as a murder suspect yet, Mr. Walsh. I need a lot more information to complete my preliminary investigation. Its outcome will decide whether or not we believe something untoward may have happened to Miss Bartelli, and it will identify any suspects that should be pursued."

"Is that reason enough to break up my marriage?" Walsh pleaded.

"I can't promise you anything of course, but I have no desire to create a rift between you and your wife. I'm only interested in finding out what has happened to Miss Bartelli."

"I guess I'll have to rely on your discretion," said Walsh with mock sarcasm.

"Goodbye, Mr. Walsh," Tanner replied, extending his hand. Walsh refused his offer, and remained silent and seated. "We'll be in touch."

Tanner smiled ominously as he left the study. Francesca was waiting in the hall to show Tanner to the front door. As he made his way to the underground car park below the apartment block, he picked over the points raised in his interview with Walsh. He was amazed that he had agreed to talk to him so freely and had expected that he would need to go to the NYPD for the authority to question him. Walsh had become agitated when asked directly about his knowledge of Elsa's disappearance and couldn't have expected any type of confrontation in the questioning. He was unconcerned at the start of the interview, but his anxiety gradually built up when it dawned on him that he was under suspicion.

The earlier picture the detective had built up of Walsh from delving into police records and his discussions with the witnesses was of a selfish, arrogant man with a complete disregard for other people, particularly women who were simply objects to him. After meeting him, he had now developed a vehement dislike for the man. He knew that it would be unprofessional to let his personal feelings for Walsh influence his recommendation on whether there was sufficient evidence to set up an arraignment hearing and begin the process of prosecuting him for murder, but he felt Walsh's behavior indicated he had something to hide.

The department already had the makings of a good case against him for the murder of Elsa. The blood and hair samples taken from his boat were damning evidence of foul play, but without a body, it would be more difficult to convince a jury of her murder. Luckily, Joe had not acted on Walsh's order to clean the boat after his return, and the police were able to get unfettered access to it on the Tuesday afternoon. Forensic investigation of the boat was bound to come up with more evidence, if a murder had been committed, which Walsh had overlooked, and could provide hard facts in the case against him.

In weighing up the prospects of a successful prosecution, Tanner thought that because Walsh was unaware of the developing case profile and the supporting evidence being collected, and based on his attitude during the interview, he would be in denial about the possibility of having a murder charge to answer. On the evidence of the interview, Walsh's arrogance would make him vulnerable as he was unlikely to offer a robust counter argument to explain events on the boat, and could even incriminate himself when charged. It was an unusual case without overwhelming evidence to prove his guilt or innocence, but in his gut, Tanner felt he was guilty.

10:

GET BACK

Jack hired a car at Miami Airport, and Elsa and he drove back to New York. Julie flew back to ensure that her return alone became a matter of record. Jack knew he would have to go to see Roland, and thought he would go straight away after settling Elsa into his apartment. They hadn't driven at a fast pace, just in case they were stopped by a bored traffic cop, and broke the journey down into three stages, each being less than 500 miles, with two overnight stops at motels. He had paid in cash — standard procedure when they were hustling — and had also used false identities. The hire car, gas and motel stops were also paid for in cash to avoid using his credit card. Luckily, Roland had sent him enough money to give Al his second payment and to deal with incidentals for Elsa, Julie and himself.

"I'm going over to the Blue Cockatoo," Jack told Elsa as she made herself comfortable on his sofa, sipping fresh mango juice.

Jack and Elsa had spent three days in a car together driving back to New York, and were both pleased by the chance of spending a little time by themselves.

"Ha! The wanderer returns!" Bannister exclaimed as Jack entered his office at the Blue Cockatoo. "What would you like to drink?"

"I'll have a cold beer in the bottle," Jack replied as he made himself comfortable on the couch. The two-way mirror gave a perfect view of the club's catwalk and bars. It was interesting to note the different expressions on the faces of the patrons as they watched the girls' parade in front of them. Some were like little boys who had just found some money in their pocket they didn't know was there. Others were overtly lustful toward the girls, but knew that they would be in big trouble if they so much as touched them. The majority were there to get drunk, gawk at the bodies on display, and tell each other what they would like to do to them given the chance.

The catwalk zigzagged through the main room of the club, forming large table areas at every change in direction. Each table area was big enough for two girls to dance, and included a pole. There were five areas for dancing and the customers gathered around the area where their favorite girl was performing. Elsa always had one of the end areas where more people could congregate around the dance floor, and when not on stage, always performed alone. The other girls didn't mind as they conceded she drew the largest crowds.

The main bar was at the far end of the room, and there was a smaller cocktail bar in the center of the longest stretch of the catwalk. The spirits were the cheapest available and the beer was weak. Nobody complained about the quality of the drinks being served or the exorbitant prices charged. Off to the side of the main area, there were small rooms that could be used for private performances.

Roland Bannister had built on the success of the place since taking it over, and certainly, appeared to know what his customers wanted. He was constantly changing the dance themes, and even had the girls play out little tableaus from time to time that simulated most of the major male sexual fantasies. Elsa didn't usually participate in this part of the entertainment or give private performances, but that seemed to make the clientele want her even more.

Jack turned to Roland Bannister to take the bottle of beer he handed him. He perceived Bannister to be the antithesis of himself both in appearance and manner, and wondered if his roots went back to one of the rich aristocratic families of

England, or maybe his ancestors were rich plantation owners involved in the slave trade. After all, Roland was still pedaling flesh, albeit in a voyeuristic way.

It was a far cry from Bannister's beginning as an attorney in a smart Manhattan law firm, where he had never quite fitted in. He was too slick and smart for the senior partners because of his success rate and the volume of work he was able to get through. He was eventually compromised in a fraud case, involving insider trading and offshore bank accounts, when the prosecution discovered he had also been investing in the same companies as his client. There was insufficient evidence to bring a criminal prosecution against him, but he was taken off the case, and dismissed by the senior partners of the law firm, who were pleased to see him go.

After that, he set up his own law practice above a betting shop in the Bronx. He had few of the trappings of most law practices, other than a brass nameplate on his office door and his framed diploma on the wall. Early clients were not business men or corporate firms, but petty criminals and people with broken marriages. Nevertheless, he confirmed the talent he had shown earlier with an exceptional success rate, and soon came to the attention of organized crime through Leonard Tuzio. They formed a steady working relationship, and Tuzio became one of his best clients. Ultimately, Bannister had arranged for the disappearance of Tuzio, who was in imminent danger of becoming another statistic at the city morgue after falling out with Mario Pallacio. He kept his client in a safe place, providing him with a new identity and passport.

Shortly after Tuzio's disappearance, Bannister took charge of the Blue Cockatoo. It was already a thriving concern that had begun life as a seedy strip club. Tuzio had changed its image, but Bannister was determined to improve on the diversity of the entertainment, ambience and image of the club, which would increase profits. After extensive refurbishment, he reopened the club in a blaze of free publicity after he had the girls do an exotic routine on a mock-up stage in front of the premises. He was arrested, but the media coverage was invaluable. Roland gave up his law practice two weeks after the club opened.

"Beer is not what successful men drink. Why don't you try and get used to some of the finer things in life? After all, we're both on the verge of making some serious money," said Bannister.

"Everybody wants more money, but they don't always need it. You already wear tailored shirts and Armani suits, and walk about in handmade shoes. Besides, I'm only drinking the beverage that befits my station in life."

"This is a celebration, Jack. Soon you'll know what it's like to have to count the number of digits on your bank statement and be able to dress like a gentleman. There was a time I thought my influence might have a positive effect on you. But somehow, I don't think it'll matter how much money you have; you'll always be a slob."

"Thank you for that, Roland. It's nice to know you hold me in such high regard. Didn't your mother tell you that clothes do not make the man, contrary to popular opinion?"

"Let's not fall out about it, Jack. Neither of us will care one way or the other when we get our hands on Walsh's money."

"We can't be certain of that until Walsh is sent down. You know better than me that he has to go to an arraignment hearing before a trial can take place, and even then, things can go wrong in a court room," Jack reasoned.

"I know that! You don't have to teach your granny to suck eggs," Roland replied, annoyed at Jack trying to dampen his enthusiasm. "If the DA thinks there's sufficient evidence for Walsh to be charged, he will take it to arraignment, and the judge presiding over the hearing will decide whether there's a case to answer. If it goes to arraignment, we can gauge how committed the police are to take the case to court."

"OK. I didn't mean to quote legal chapter and verse to a lawyer, and I wasn't trying to take the wind out of your sails.

I just think we've got to tread carefully and take things slowly. We have a good chance of success, but we'll need to make sure events outside our control are kept to a minimum. Without a body, the forensic evidence and integrity of the witnesses will be crucial in convincing the judge that Walsh should go to trial."

"I've been trying to find out who the DA's assigned as lead lawyer for the prosecution from Gene Tanner," Jack continued. "A few attorneys think it will be a high-profile case so there'll be a race to get it, but it will probably be James Bantry, who has a good hit rate."

"Bantry spent his early career in New York, and I helped him out of a jam when we both worked in the same law firm. He could be an ally," Roland replied.

"Gene has told me that the DNA of the blood found on Walsh's boat matches Elsa's of course, as do the hair samples. It was lucky the mechanic ignored Walsh's instruction to wash the deck. But we're both overlooking one major thing that will work against Walsh; that is that he really thinks he's guilty of a crime. That will affect the way he handles himself in court, even if it is just his body language. He believes he murdered Elsa."

"Don't forget the gun, Jack. If the DA finds out Walsh used a gun to intimidate Elsa, and it was actually fired, the stakes go up considerably. It doesn't matter if he's charged with second-degree murder or manslaughter, the use of a gun will put at least 10 years onto his sentence, if he's found guilty," Bannister added. "The problem is, it could be a double-edged sword. If Walsh decides the stakes are too high not to stick with a murder plea, he'd be charged with Elsa's attempted murder after she shows up, which would remove any incentive to pay us."

"Don't worry, he won't be harassed into making a confession. After all, there were no witnesses to the actual shooting, except Elsa, and she's supposed to be dead! He'll keep quiet and expect to ride it out," Jack replied.

"Well, then, why aren't you a little more optimistic about the outcome? I've seen successful cases prosecuted with far less going for them than this one. Lighten up, you've got me worried that I'm not going to recoup my little investment, which is growing daily by the way."

"C'mon, Roland! 20 grand is nothing to you. It's just spare change, you must be a millionaire by now."

"The money doesn't concern me, Jack; it's the winning that's important. I've always been a winner no matter how heavily the odds were stacked against me. Even when I was kicked out of Farnshaw and Blythe, I came up smelling of roses. So I'm not changing to the losing side now."

"I agree, but nothing's guaranteed in this life. All we can do is lay the groundwork as professionally as possible and hope the plan pans out as expected."

"Well, why don't we go for the short odds and make a deal for Elsa to show before they bring the case to court?" Bannister suggested.

"No," Jack rasped. "We won't be able to ask for anything like the amount of money I want. Money may not be important to you, Roland, but it is to me. This deal is going to be my last, and will make me enough to kiss goodbye to creeping around the sewers of New York."

"C'mon, Jack! You know that you can't make that kind of decision on your own. It's my money at stake not yours."

"Look, Roland. I know that we're a team and decisions have to be made together," Jack replied impatiently, "but we're in too good a position to throw it all away. Walsh is in a tight spot and I'm sure that he's beginning to understand his problem. All we've got to do is sit tight and let things develop."

"That's exactly what I've been saying! Cool down, Jack! I was only trying to make a point. I know you've got this thing planned out in your head, but you've got to let Elsa and me know what's going on. We're all partners and have an equal say in how to manage this deal. Don't worry. I agree with you that it's far better to wait."

Jack was too intent in his desire to convince Bannister of the benefits of his scheme to be aware that his partner had been toying with him. Bannister enjoyed taking the contrary position in any argument, which was probably down to his training as an attorney. The two men continued to analyze the case until the early hours of the morning. They concluded that Bantry should be tactfully pointed toward carrying out forensic tests on Walsh's gun. This knowledge would confirm if the gun had been fired recently, adding great strength to the case against Walsh.

Although Jack normally enjoyed the banter he shared with Bannister, this time he was annoyed his partner had continued the role-playing for the fun of it. More importantly, he became aware for the first time that the cool business image projected by Bannister camouflaged the true character of a very ruthless man. So far, Bannister had given Jack a lot of slack to let him operate in any way he saw fit, partly because he respected Jack's judgement but also because of his own infatuation with Elsa; if, however, things went wrong, he would be a very difficult man to placate.

11:

JACK

Jack regretted having shown Bannister his private side in expressing his desire to escape his humdrum existence and the racket he was in. He didn't want Bannister to know how much the success of this job meant to him, thinking it would weaken his position in the partnership. Bannister could afford the diversion of playing his little mind games, but he wanted to remain focused until the job was over. He was not the same man who had joined the NYPD 15 years earlier as a naïve idealist.

Jack had gone to university on a sport scholarship through playing football. At one time, he had considered turning professional, but a torn meniscus in his left knee took away that opportunity. His father was a policeman with the NYPD, and suggested he join the force when he left university. Jack's potential was quickly recognized by his superiors, and after a brief period in uniform he was given training as a detective and assigned to homicide. He quickly progressed to the rank of detective sergeant, and gained a reputation both on the street and in his precinct as a fair and honest cop.

Proud of his reputation, Jack continued to operate efficiently without internal conflict with his peers in the force or interference from his superiors. His one-dimensional view of the criminal world and the role he played in containing it remained with him until he got involved in the investigation of the murder of a young prostitute with his partner Charlie Inglewood. Her death was neither shocking nor unexpected, as the word on the street was that she had crossed her pimp

Enrique Gonzales and taken up with a rival. Neither pimp had any saving graces that would commend them to her, so the reason behind her taking the risk of moving from one to the other was far from obvious, and one which she took to her grave. Her mutilated body could only be identified from dental records. She was tied in a loving embrace to the body of her new pimp, who had also been tortured. The tableau Gonzales had left in a seedy hotel room was a warning to his other girls not to cross him.

A tip-off led Jack and Charlie to another hotel in Harlem only two blocks from the murder scene. Gonzales was arrogant and never considered the consequences of his actions or a need to keep a low profile following the discovery of the bodies. Screams were heard from one of the upstairs rooms where a prostitute was entertaining a client. Jack knew from her identification by the desk clerk that the woman was one of Gonzales's girls and that Gonzales, who felt the need to keep the women working for him in a constant state of fear, often visited her. The john had been seen running from the hotel room, half dressed and with a bleeding lip. Shouting and then screams followed his exit and the desk clerk reluctantly called the police.

After confirming the hotel room number, Jack took the elevator to the second floor, while Charlie took the stairs. As he emerged from the elevator, the sound of gunshots rose up through the staircase. He raced toward the sound and on opening the door to the landing, found Charlie being held as a shield in front of Gonzales, who was pointing a gun at his head. The pimp smiled when he saw Jack and squeezed off a shot in his general direction. Jack fell backward into the corridor and quickly scrambled a retreat, out of view. He heard the squeaking hinges of the door onto the first-floor corridor, and followed cautiously. Gonzales was a giant of a man and the strength in his arm was throttling Charlie; his face was red and the veins in his temples were standing out. He again smiled at

Jack when he appeared, but this time he kept his gun pointed at Charlie's head.

"Stop where you are unless you want your partner to get his head blown off!" Gonzales shouted. Jack was about 25 feet away from Gonzales and held his gun in both hands pointed directly at the pimp's head. "You might get lucky and kill me, but will it be before I kill him?" the pimp said, smiling and nodding toward Charlie.

"Kill him and you'll be dead before he hits the floor."

"Well, in that case we have a stalemate," Gonzales said, smiling, "'cause if you take me in, I'll get life anyway, so I ain't got much to lose, do I?"

Jack was lost for a response. "Put your gun down..." he stuttered.

"No! You put your gun down motherfucker or he dies now!"

For a brief second, Jack thought he might get a shot off, but he couldn't be sure of not hitting Charlie. Police protocol was never to give up your weapon, but unable to see a way of saving his partner, he decided to drop his gun rather than risk Charlie's life.

"Now kick it over here," the pimp demanded.

Grudgingly, Jack did as he was told. As the gun came to rest at the pimp's feet Jack watched incredulously as Gonzales squeezed the trigger of the gun he was holding. The trigger clicked harmlessly and Charlie nearly fainted. Gonzales smiled again at Jack, pulled a knife from the sleeve of the arm he had around Charlie's neck, grabbed his captive's hair with his other hand and calmly slit his throat.

Jack felt rooted to the ground as blood spurted out of Charlie's neck, unable to stop the pimp from murdering his partner. His muscles suddenly jerked back into life and he rushed toward Gonzales, but before he had made three steps toward his target, the pimp picked up Jack's gun and fired it at him. Jack was hit in the stomach and collapsed before his momentum could carry him to a position where he could grab hold of the pimp, and he feebly flailed at air, falling face down.

Gonzales turned Jack over onto his back. Jack winced with the pain caused by his movement and covered his wound with both hands. "That looks painful" said Gonzales with an unsympathetic sneer. He put his foot on top of Jack's hands and pressed down. Jack screamed in pain and doubled up around the pimp's foot. Gonzales lifted his foot and Jack fell back onto the floor.

Jack looked up into the face of Gonzales, who was now pointing the gun at his head.

"Go on, then, you bastard! Shoot!" he shouted deliriously.

At that moment, the noise of sirens filled the air as several police cars pulled up outside the hotel. "You're already a dead man," said Gonzales before he disappeared through the staircase exit as Jack saw a red mist descend over his eyes.

Three minutes later, armed policemen burst onto the first-floor corridor, and found Jack unconscious. He was taken to the Mount Sinai Hospital and given emergency surgery to have the bullet removed and stop the internal bleeding. He was moved into intensive care after the operation, and at one stage during the first night, came very close to death, because of the amount of blood he had lost.

The pain Jack endured from the gunshot wound was insignificant compared to the guilt he felt over Charlie's murder. He had helped Gonzales kill Charlie and escape by handing over his gun so easily. In the police academy and during his early days on the force, he had been repeatedly told never to hand over his firearm no matter what the situation. Nobody had told him how to handle the dilemma of either letting Charlie die or stopping Gonzales, because he didn't believe he could do both. Looking into Charlie's eyes, Jack had to shoulder the burden of trust placed on him by his partner. The only time Charlie had shown fear was when Jack laid down his gun. At the academy, everything was clear-cut, and in the staged scenarios, they used to teach the students there was no undue concern about the obligation to protect others in the handling of such situations. In reality, the edges get blurred, especially when a friend's life is at stake.

Jack handed in his badge to the NYPD while he was still in hospital, and used his outstanding vacation leave to cover the balance of the notice required to quit the job. There was no fuss or leaving party on his departure. He simply never went back to the precinct station. He kept his contacts with the NYPD, and they helped him operate as a private investigator, giving him an edge the competition didn't have. It was through one of these contacts he got a lead on the whereabouts of Gonzales one cold, wet November night.

Despite an intense manhunt, Gonzales remained elusive. The police had put tails on some of his girls, but he still managed a covert control over them, and got his end of the action. He had been seen with one of his girls in the same hotel where he had murdered Charlie. One of Pat O'Connor's snitches had passed on the information after bumping into him in the lobby. Pat was Charlie's brother in law, and a close friend of Jack. Rather than report the sighting to homicide, Pat immediately told Jack and they both went over to the hotel to verify the sighting. After confirmation of his room number, Pat kept watch outside the hotel while Jack climbed up to Gonzales's room on the fire escape. Jack prized open the window as quietly as he could and found Gonzales sleeping in bed next to his girl. She was awake, her eyes puffy from crying and her lips bruised. As Jack climbed through the window, she remained silent, holding her gaze as he came to the bed. He pulled out a switchblade from his pocket and released the catch. The girl remained impassive as the knife sprang out of its holder, and never flinched as Jack placed the blade on Gonzales throat and stabbed downward across one half of his neck, cutting his artery. Gonzales immediately started retching, grabbing hold of his throat, as if he was trying to stop the torrent of blood from gushing outward. Jack's smiling face was the last image Gonzales saw before he lost consciousness.

After she was sure he was dead, the girl next to Gonzales sprang from the bed, went around to the opposite side where Jack was standing, and spat on the pimp's face. Jack pulled her away from the bed and told her to get dressed and leave. Even though he had avenged Charlie's death, Jack never lost the feeling of guilt from having capitulated to Gonzales.

12:

FIRST CRACKS

As Jack entered his apartment, he was still mulling over the wisdom of including Roland Bannister in the deal, but couldn't see any other way as he didn't have the cash to finance it himself. Bannister had been easily drawn in because of his infatuation with Elsa, but Jack didn't want to capitalize on it. She had been through enough already without adding to her problems by kindling fires within Bannister that could lead to an awkward situation in the future. Jack now knew that despite his education and apparent refinement, Bannister had a dark side to his personality that was not too far beneath the smooth, sophisticated surface he showed to the world.

One thing Jack had learned from his years in the police force was that unscrupulous men do unscrupulous things. He remembered his early days with homicide and being physically sick at the scene of his first murder enquiry after seeing the state of the murder victim. It was a young boy who had been kidnapped and raped. In an attempt to disguise the identity of the boy, the murderer had cut off his hands and his head. In a perverse act, the murderer had also removed his genitals, merely to satisfy himself. The skull of the boy was found in the furnace used for heating the building where the body was discovered.

Jack was sure that Bannister could be capable of murder. He had seen him pistol-whip a drunken customer who had tried to grab one of the girls in the club, caving in the cheekbone of the unfortunate man. When Jack had suggested he had been a little severe, Bannister conceded that he might have acted brutally and without any sign of emotion, but only because the girls were his business assets and he had to protect them; his business, which he was protecting. The obvious lack of consideration for the physical damage he caused his victim was a familiar trait that Jack had witnessed in a number of evildoers who were at a loss to understand the concern shown by others over the consequences of their vicious acts.

The apartment was dimly lit up by the signs in the street. In the half-light, Jack made his way to the bedroom. He took off his jacket and threw it on a chair next to the dressing table. Looking over toward the bed, he could see Elsa sprawled diagonally across it, face down, hugging the pillow. The bed sheet was draped across the bed in the opposite direction, and revealed tantalizing glimpses of her body. The part of the bed sheet that covered her, clung to every curve. He stared at her silently, amazed that the sight of Elsa's half-naked body still gave him as big a thrill as on the first night he had seen her performing at the Blue Cockatoo.

He took off his shoes and gently got onto the bed, and lay behind Elsa. He put his hand on her bare shoulder, and ran it down her back, pulling down the bed sheet at the same time. Elsa made no move toward Jack, leaving him puzzled as he didn't know whether she was asleep or awake. He stood up and pulled the bed sheet down the full length of the bed, still without a sound from Elsa. She turned on her side, clutching the pillow, and the sight of her naked body aroused him even more. He climbed back into the bed and lay behind her, and he put his arm around her waist to draw her closer to him.

Feeling the lower half of Elsa's breast, he followed its curve down to her torso and over her flat belly. Elsa kept herself in shape and beneath her silky-smooth skin he could feel the ripple of her abdominal muscles. His hand wandered to the fleshy, velvety mound between her legs and he caressed her gently. Elsa sighed quietly half turning away from him, to return to her original position and lie on her front. Jack still couldn't decide if she was awake or just instinctively responding to his touch in her sleep. He kissed the back of her neck and began caressing her body again moving closer to her. He now felt he wanted her so badly that it almost hurt.

He began to be more adventurous with his kisses and caresses, fondling Elsa's right breast and kissing her neck and shoulders, still reluctant to turn her toward him. If she was asleep, he didn't want to wake her suddenly by pulling her onto her back. He wanted her to awaken by herself, aroused by his fondling, and turn toward him as anxious to make love as he was. He was now up against her body and could feel her behind pressing into his groin. He was beginning to get a little exasperated at Elsa's lack of response when she softly said, "When are you going to stop playing about and give me what I need?"

Jack turned her sharply toward him and kissed her passionately on the mouth. Elsa started unbuttoning his shirt and loosening the belt on his trousers. Within a few seconds, Jack was naked next to Elsa. Every time they made love, it felt exciting, almost as if it were the first time and they were still finding out about each other. Jack had been with several women but none had come close to making him feel the way Elsa did. He couldn't remember what sex had been like before he had first slept with her, and now he didn't care to remember.

After they had made love, Elsa went over to the fridge pulled out a bottle of Chardonnay and opened it. She returned to the bed with the bottle and two wine glasses. Jack sat up, took the glasses from Elsa, and let her fill each of them.

"You should've just got me a cold bottle of Bud," said Jack.

"The sight of you with a beer bottle stuck out of your mouth is not very romantic. Besides, I wouldn't do this with a bottle of Bud," Elsa replied pouring some wine onto her breasts.

Jack leaned over to catch the rivulets of wine running down Elsa's body, lingering on her breasts after the wine had gone.

"Stop it, Jack! That's enough, or you're going to make me spill the rest of my wine."

"I'll never complain about drinking wine again. Why can't we put the wine on one side and make love again?"

"Because I want to talk about Walsh."

"What! We've just made love and you want to talk about another man."

"Don't be so crass, Jack. Believe me I don't find that the least bit funny," Elsa replied sternly.

Jack sat up at being made aware he had been insensitive.

"I'm sorry, baby. I didn't mean…"

"I know you're just a man and able to pass over what happened in Miami very quickly! It will take more than a few days for me to get over what he did, or tried to do. When I think of what could have happened, it frightens me. I've never really thought of myself as being a victim before, but now I know I'm no different to anyone else."

Jack realized he had been insensitive, even though he was simply trying to lighten the subject. He took her hand and squeezed it, signaling his support and letting her carry on to make her point.

"We do have to talk about him. I'm a prisoner in your apartment because I can't be seen and we don't even know if the DA plans to bring a case against him."

"The Miami police sent someone to interview Walsh in New York. They must think there's more to your disappearance than meets the eye, otherwise they wouldn't bother going to such trouble simply to get a statement. They'd get someone from New York to conduct the interview and send the statement down to them."

"Look, Jack. I can't stay here indefinitely; I've only been a couple of days in the apartment and its driving me crazy already!"

"If the police drop the case, we'll make up some story for your reappearance, but if they decide Walsh has a case to answer at the arraignment, we'll move you out of New York so you can have a bit more freedom to move around."

"And that's supposed to make me feel better? I had a life, Jack, no matter what you may think of it. I might as well be dead the way I'm living now."

Jack reached out to comfort Elsa, but she brushed his hand off her shoulder, and lifted the wine glass to her mouth. The earlier sexual excitement they had generated together had been dissipated and was replaced with a cold tension. They drew a mutual halt to the conversation, not wishing to exacerbate the darkness that had grown between them, almost as if Walsh had walked into the room. It was the first crack in their relationship since becoming lovers.

13:

QUIZ BRIDGET

"I'm glad you were able to meet me at such short notice," said Detective Tanner as he greeted Bridget Walsh. Tanner had suggested they meet in a coffee shop because it would be more discreet than him going to the NMP offices. The place he had selected for their meeting was only a short distance from her workplace.

"When you said you wished to discuss in private a matter my husband was involved in during his vacation in Miami, I was too worried and intrigued not to meet you," Bridget replied, taking a seat across the table from Tanner.

"Would you like a coffee?" Tanner asked.

"Thank you. I'll have an espresso."

Tanner called over the waitress and ordered an espresso for Bridget. "I told Simon I would be speaking to you without being too specific. Have you told him you were coming to meet me today?"

"You asked me not to when we arranged the meeting," Bridget replied, not answering Tanner's question directly and leaving him no wiser. "I don't know what the secrecy is about, but I did what you wanted."

"I didn't want him to influence what you might say to me," said Tanner, now knowing that the interview was not going to be easy. He decided he might just as well be direct, rather than trying to fence with Bridget. It was obvious she was too intelligent to be manipulated in the same way as her husband. "Does your husband often take vacations by himself?" he asked.

"He goes down to Florida about the same time every year for the sailing and golf, neither of which I particularly enjoy. We've been married long enough not to live in each other's pockets."

Tanner had looked into the background of the Walsh marriage. Happily married men don't pick up women in bars. "But according to the hotel he normally stays at, you and your husband have never been on vacation together. In fact, after digging further, I found out, your honeymoon only lasted one day."

"Don't judge me and my husband by the standards you set yourself. We like different types of vacation and can afford to holiday separately. Besides, we are together at work and at home and it does us good to take a break from each other. I don't understand what significance our vacation arrangements have on your inquiry. Can we get to the point?"

"Separate vacations, and the way your husband behaves down in Florida, indicates either your marriage is platonic, or he is dissatisfied, which is very relevant to my inquiry. Did you know that your husband was with a young woman called Elsa Bartelli last Friday, and she has not been seen since going out with him on his boat?"

"First of all, don't be surprised when I tell you that my husband often meets young women when he's on his own. I don't mind, provided he behaves discreetly and doesn't bring his habits back to New York," said Bridget coldly.

This didn't come as any surprise, as Tanner could see Bridget was the dominant partner in their marriage. "That's very understanding of you. Do you have what they call an open marriage?"

"I'm sure we each have secrets we hide from one another, but none that would affect our marriage."

"Does that mean you meet young men when you go on vacation?"

"I can see you're only able to think in straight lines, Detective; that must be very limiting in your job," Bridget replied sarcastically.

Tanner ignored the rebuke, "Are you trying to avoid answering my question?"

"No. What I do on vacation is not pertinent to your inquiry and is none of your damn business."

Tanner couldn't visualize Mr. and Mrs. Walsh together. She was strong, bright and tenacious, qualities alien to her husband.

"Yes, you're right it's none of my business. The hotel records show that your husband rang you on Friday evening. What did the two of you talk about?"

"Well, we didn't talk about his latest conquest, if that's what you mean? He made a quick call to see how I was and tell me he'd been out sailing. Nothing more, nothing less."

"At what time did he call you?" Tanner asked.

"It was about 7:30 p.m. He said he had returned to the hotel feeling unwell and had gone to bed for a rest before calling me. The hotel records should support me."

"We've checked your husband's movements at both the marina and the hotel. He spoke to the mechanic at the marina at 6:45 p.m. and checked in at the hotel at 7:10 p.m. It doesn't appear as if he was able to get much sleep, does it?"

For the first time, Tanner noticed a trace of doubt cross Bridget's face. She looked away from him, trying to find a good reason that would justify Simon lying to her, and weighing up the possibility that he could be involved in something even darker. Bridget couldn't understand why Simon would need to resort to doing anything unlawful. He had money to pay for the kind of woman he usually associated with on these trips, and past experience seemed to indicate he wasn't too fussy in his choices.

"If you knew his movements, why did you need to see me?"

"I'm just tying up loose ends to confirm that he did in fact speak to you when he made the telephone call. It closes the loop and gives credence to the timings given in the statements of the other witnesses."

"I think you're hoping for more than that. You would like me to go back to my husband with all guns blazing to put him under more pressure, or even get him to do something rash."

"You're making the assumption that we suspect him of injuring or killing Miss Bartelli. Do you think he would be capable of such an act?"

"You have a slick way of turning the conversation to your own advantage," Bridget said, smiling, "but no, I don't think he would be capable of murder."

"I am experienced in these types of interview, and I don't think you know your husband as well as you think. Ask him about Rita Alonso. She's the prostitute he very nearly killed in New Orleans. She refused to submit to him, and he hit her so hard, she was in a coma for two days. But if you want to blind yourself to what he could be capable of, that's your prerogative. Thank you for your time," said Tanner as he rose to leave. "Oh, one more thing, Mrs. Walsh. Does your husband own a gun, and does he normally take it on vacation with him?"

Bridget was still reeling from Tanner's reference to Rita Alonso, but his question about Simon owning a gun brought her thoughts sharply back into focus. "Yes, he takes it down to Florida with him. He started taking it with him after he found a tramp sleeping on his boat a couple of years ago. Surely, he didn't shoot this woman."

"She's missing and there's no physical evidence to go on. Consequently, I have to consider every possibility from A to Z. Thanks again for your time." With that, Tanner walked off, leaving Bridget in a very confused state.

Bridget's own experience of Simon was enough to tell her that he was a man with little moral fiber, but she hadn't thought him capable of seriously injuring or killing someone. The thought of him as a murderer made her feel very vulnerable, but she couldn't equate the spineless man who had meekly accepted her terms for their marriage on their wedding night to a cold-blooded killer. If anything had happened to Elsa Bartelli, she was convinced it was due to an accident. What had the stupid man done?

Bridget was waiting for her husband that evening as he entered the study.

"It's a surprise to find you in here. I'm having a drink. Do you want one?" he asked, walking over to the drinks cabinet.

"No, thanks, Simon. I've been talking to Detective Tanner of the MPD as he felt we needed to discuss your vacation."

"Yes, he said he was going to talk to you, but I expected him to come back to our apartment."

"I didn't speak to him here. We met downtown and he had quite a story to tell. Who is this Elsa Bartelli and did you have any involvement in her disappearance?"

"Don't be ridiculous. I barely knew the woman; she came onto me in a bar and I eventually found out she was just another hooker on the game. I took her out on my boat for the afternoon in good faith, but when I found out what she was after, I didn't want any part of her."

"I hope you're telling the truth. I know you're a low, conniving, immoral excuse for a man, but if you've harmed her or played any part in her disappearance, don't expect to count on my support."

"Look. I'm the victim here. I was reeled in by a woman who was out to get whatever she could from me. She was in the Ocean Drop Inn last Friday afternoon, waiting to latch onto some high roller. I didn't catch on at first because she seemed to be a classy woman and certainly didn't look like a whore; in fact, she could have been a tourist just looking for a quiet drink on a warm afternoon."

"Well, I think you're saying she wasn't a stereotype, but nevertheless she was a whore. So, go on! What happened next?"

"I've already told you. We went out for a short trip on my boat, and that was it!"

"So, MPD have sent one of their detectives all the way to New York simply to talk to you about an innocent little boat trip? Don't lie, Simon! I know there's got to be more to it than that, and I also know about New Orleans and Rita!"

Walsh froze when Bridget mentioned Rita Alonso's name.

"Who told you…?"

"It doesn't matter who told me about her, but I've done a little investigating of my own this afternoon. In case you can't remember, she's the prostitute you nearly beat to death in a seedy New Orleans brothel!"

"You don't understand the bitch was trying to steal my money; I caught her red handed and hit her in anger. She ended up in hospital, but I didn't mean to hurt her; it was an accident."

"And what about Elsa Bartelli? Wait — don't tell me — that was another accident and you didn't mean to hurt her either, right?"

Walsh looked at Bridget, and knowing he was in desperate need of her support, realized he would have to come as close to the truth as he dared without completely losing her goodwill.

"OK. Something did happen when we were out at sea, but it wasn't something that I did. What happened was completely out of my control!"

"Don't try to elicit my sympathy before you tell the story. Just give me the facts, and let me decide about your innocence."

Walsh sat down opposite her and took a long drink of whiskey, emptying his glass. Putting the glass on the floor in front of him, he clasped his hands, trying to decide what to say and where to start. "As I said, we met in the Ocean Drop Inn. She told me she was on vacation in Miami, visiting her sister, but was on her own while her sister was at work. It was a nice day and I offered to take her out on the boat, which was being prepared for one last fishing trip before the end of my vacation."

"That was very generous of you. I guess you did it out of concern for her missing out on her holiday, and because of the innate goodness within you to show her a good time," Bridget chided.

"Alright, she was a stunner, and yes, I was immediately attracted to her. Given our relationship, I don't think it's anything for me to feel guilty about."

"OK. Carry on!" Bridget urged impatiently.

"Everything was straightforward. We got on the boat and headed out to the reef. After I dropped anchor, she changed completely. There had been a little flirting up to this point but nothing that prepared me for what followed. She took off her clothes, saying she wanted to top up her tan, and then started caressing herself suggestively. By this time, I was straining at the leash and I moved next to her and began to touch her. She didn't object and even encouraged me to go further."

"This just sounds like one of your normal vacations. When did it turn nasty?"

"It started to heat up and eventually I said I would get a condom from below deck. I returned to find her with my wallet in her hand, stuffing money and credit cards into her handbag. I took the wallet from her and slapped her across her face. She went berserk, scratching and spitting, and for some reason ended up jumping overboard."

"Why would she do that?"

"It must have been because I threatened to call the police when we got back to the marina."

"Didn't you try to get her back into the boat?"

"I wasn't able to because when I went to the side of the boat, I couldn't see her in the water. I searched along both sides of the boat before giving up. Then I started to panic. I saw myself in the very predicament that seems to be developing now. I know I'm innocent, but I won't be able to convince anyone else. You do believe me, don't you?"

"Is that why you didn't go to the MPD and make a statement?"

"With my background, there wasn't a chance in hell they would believe me, and I'd be in a cell now."

Bridget simply nodded her head in support. She wanted to believe Simon, but knew what an accomplished liar he could be. "Don't let me find out that you're lying," she warned again, "because I can do a lot of damage if this thing goes to court." Bridget suddenly felt that she couldn't bear to be in the same room as Simon. She got out of her chair and left without another word.

As she went up the stairs to her bedroom, Bridget tried to be positive about the story she had just been given by Simon. She knew she could never be certain about his involvement in Elsa Bartelli's disappearance, but cold-heartedly consoled herself in the thought that he could never attract a woman of real substance.

14:

THE WOLF

Elsa opened the apartment door to see the smiling face of Roland Bannister staring back at her as he handed her a bottle of champagne.

"Why, thank you, Roland. What's the occasion?"

"Just seeing you is cause enough to celebrate, especially as I hardly get to see you now that you're hiding out here and not coming to the club anymore. I'm missing you, and so are my customers."

"I'm sure there are plenty of other girls for them to drool over. They'll soon forget me," Elsa replied, taking the bottle of champagne and walking into the apartment. She put the bottle on the coffee table in the center of the lounge and went into the kitchen to fetch a couple of glasses.

"No, you're their favorite, so they won't easily forget you. Your story was given a brief airing in the *New York Herald*, and I've already had several people tell me what they're going to do to Simon Walsh if you don't turn up soon."

"Wait a minute, Roland! I can't hear you!" Elsa shouted from the kitchen.

Bannister sat down in one of the two easy chairs. "You don't give yourself enough credit, Elsa. You're the unattainable woman that they all want but will never get because you have too much class to mix with the rabble at the club. They'll never feel the same toward any of the other girls because they don't have that extra indefinable something that naturally seeps from every pore in your skin."

"Steady, Roland. Slow down or else I'll think that you're trying to make a move on me," said Elsa, putting the flutes on the table in front of Bannister, alongside the champagne.

"What if I am?" said Roland, picking up the bottle and starting to loosen the cork. "You could do a lot worse than me. I'd treat you far better than Jack, and I wouldn't expect you to keep putting your neck on the line for those two-bit scams of his."

"Well, after this little episode, believe me I won't be doing it again," Elsa replied.

The cork popped out of the bottle, and the champagne gushed a little before Bannister started pouring it into the glasses. He handed Elsa one of the glasses.

"I know it's a little early but I really need this drink," said Elsa, taking a sip from the glass and feeling the effervescence explode on her tongue. "It's been so boring holed up in Jack's apartment, I'm slowly going crazy."

"Where's Jack?" Bannister asked.

"He's always got something to do, and that leaves me stuck here on my own all day and most of the night."

"Why do you put up with it? You know I could give you so much more."

"Well, now you're just as deeply involved in this scam as Jack and me. If I show up and get recognized, it will be blown open and you'd lose the money you've already put into it."

"I don't care about that. I'd rather see you back to your old self, away from Jack and with me. You know, you could really have been killed down in Miami? I can't believe Jack put you at such risk. What was he thinking?"

"I know, Roland, but I'm probably as much to blame as Jack for putting myself in harm's way, and not thinking of how he was going to follow me. I was overconfident."

"There's no need to protect him. It's his cockeyed schemes that put you in danger in the first place."

"I'm not. Jack has always been very professional in the way he's planned these jobs and this is the first time anything's gone wrong. He couldn't have known that Walsh is a psycho."

"I don't know how he can let other men touch you. If it were me, I wouldn't even let you dance at the club."

"Jack's always accepted what I do. Don't forget he met me at the club."

"OK. Forget about that and about Jack, and come live with me. You don't need to rely on a payout from Walsh, I'll take care of you, the way a woman like you should be treated."

"That's a lovely sentiment Roland and I know, at this moment, you really mean it, thank you. But I would eventually become just another of your trophies. You're a man of refinement and taste who likes to collect things, simply because you have the desire and money to do so. You like to be surrounded by art or anything else that you put a high value on. When my looks fade, as they will, you'll want someone young and fresh to replace me. And so, by refusing you now I'm saving you the embarrassment of discarding me later. And besides I really do love Jack in spite of his faults."

"I think that was a brush off most kindly and delicately handled," said Bannister taking her hand and kissing it, "but don't think I've given up."

"What a cozy scene!" said Jack, entering the lounge. Elsa smiled warmly at him, feeling a little relieved that Bannister's love platitudes would now go no further, however her suitor looked far from happy to see Jack. "You must have heard the good news, Roland? I guess that's why you've brought over a bottle of champagne, right?"

"What news?" Bannister asked.

"My contact down in Miami tells me that Walsh is to be arrested today and will be flown down to Florida immediately with a police guard. Have you another glass for me Elsa?"

"He won't appreciate champagne, Elsa. Just get him a Bud out of the cold box," Bannister said, sneering.

"C'mon, Roland! Be nice! We've all got a good reason to celebrate. The DA in Miami has constructed a credible case against Walsh, complete with eyewitness accounts and forensic evidence. And Walsh won't be the first guy convicted for homicide without the benefit of a dead body."

"I don't know, Jack. It's still a tough call," Bannister interjected. "There will always be that element of doubt without the body. The prosecution attorney will have to convince the judge at the arraignment hearing that there is sufficient evidence to take Walsh to trial. It relies on the testimonies of the witnesses confirming she went out with him, but never came back. That's a tall order for anyone."

"Who's being pessimistic now? Once he gets to trial, we'll be in a strong position because Walsh actually thinks he killed Elsa and has something to hide. Let's hope he decides to testify and ends up tripping himself up during the cross-examination. They haven't named the prosecutor yet, but rumor has it that it will be your friend James Bantry, Roland. He's got a fine reputation and won't pull any punches."

"I spoke to Bantry recently, and he told me he was lined up for a Puerto Rican drug-smuggling case," Bannister replied.

"Yes, he was, but that collapsed because the two main defendants were murdered when they were being transferred from their arraignment hearing back to prison," Jack replied, settling into the other easy chair and taking a bottle of Bud from Elsa.

"This could be a fortunate turn of events. As you say, Bantry is a good prosecutor, and will go for the jugular every time. If anyone can trap Walsh, he can."

"If we get through the arraignment, I think we're home and dry," Jack replied.

"Don't be too optimistic. Walsh's attorney will have him well-rehearsed. By the time they get to court, he'll have gone over his story dozens of times and he will have been coached on how to address any eventuality in a cross-examination."

"We can always hope that Bantry gets him in a tight spot and he starts to improvise. If he contradicts himself on the stand, the jury will convict him, body or no body," Jack replied.

Elsa sat down on the sofa opposite the two men. "I don't know how he's going to explain leaving the marina with me on board and returning alone. Surely, that fact in itself is going to raise a significant doubt in the jury's mind. I agree with Jack. Walsh is going to have a difficult time with Bantry, and he just might end up convicting himself."

"I'm not going to argue with a lady. Let's drink to that happy outcome," said Bannister, raising his glass.

15:

ARREST

Walsh and Tanner walked onto the Miami-bound plane handcuffed together. Walsh had tried to convince Tanner to forgo putting on the handcuffs, promising to obey the detective's instructions to the letter throughout the trip. Tanner calmly refused the request, stating it was strict police procedure to use handcuffs in these circumstances for all criminal suspects, regardless of the embarrassment it might cause to the individual. While the detective's sympathetic tone of voice sounded authentic, Walsh couldn't help noticing the relish with which Tanner had shackled him. On arrival, the two men made their way to the terminal building of Miami airport, and once inside, headed directly to the police car that Tanner knew would be waiting at the exit.

The walk through the arrivals terminal to the police car was intense as they had to run a gauntlet of TV and newspaper reporters and a throng of rabid freelance photographers. The paparazzi pushed against each other, eager to get marketable shots of Walsh in cuffs, and forced their way to the front of the crowd. At one stage, all Walsh could see was a blinding bank of camera flashes flaring in quick succession. He put his free hand up to his face to protect his eyes, and grimaced, complaining to Tanner about the intrusion on his privacy. The reporters made up the second wave of attack, equally determined to get some sort of statement from him, making their progress through the terminal feel like an excruciatingly-slow picture reel. Initially, they addressed Walsh directly, quizzing him on the whereabouts of Elsa, but getting no response, they turned on Tanner to ask the policeman if they were intending to charge him.

By now, Walsh's infamy was creating a level of media interest normally reserved for a visiting celebrity. All the local papers had been running Elsa's story since she was first reported missing to the police. Her face was everywhere. Jack had directed Julie to visit the offices of the *Herald*, the most prominent of the local rags, instructing her to furnish their star reporter with a broad outline of Elsa's trip with Walsh and her subsequent disappearance. He felt Elsa's colorful background was juicy enough to generate press interest, and he was right — it did. The paper wasted no time in asking Roland Bannister for publicity stills of Elsa, which he gladly provided, lapping up the attention that came with it. After the initial report of her disappearance, the natural momentum of the police investigation was monitored by the paper, which churned out further reports to update readers, refreshing public interest. By the time Walsh arrived at Miami airport, his arrest was front page in every paper in Florida.

The detective and the prisoner had been protected from the frenzied reporters by uniformed Miami police officers at the airport, but Walsh was still horrified at the raw intensity of the media interest in his case. In the car, he remembered being arrested for his assault on Rita Alonso, but that hadn't created a fraction of the attention he was now experiencing. Naively, Walsh was unaware his father had stopped the press from revealing his sleazy misdemeanor by trading it for a bigger story on insider dealing on the New York stock market. Seán Walsh was well respected by the press, and he fully understood the nature and extent of the serious flaws in the moral character of his son. For a long time, Seán had resorted to relying on the confidence of old and trusted friends in the media and beyond to provide a protective blanket around his child, and that had continued until the old man's death. Now that goodwill shield was absent.

On his arrival at police headquarters, Walsh was taken through preliminary arraignment procedures, drearily surrendering his personal belongings and having his photograph and fingerprints taken. He was kept in the 'pound' for a few hours, while his documents were processed, before being marched down to the cells in the basement. His tiny cell was stark and dingy with a cold, iron, cot bed along the wall, a tin basin in the corner and a slop bucket below it. The police guard escorting Walsh to his cell advised him dinner would be at 5:00 (in two hours' time). The guard then left Walsh in the cell, and closed the door. Seconds later, he flipped open the hatch in the door to take a final look at Walsh, then closed it sharply before continuing his normal routine. Walsh shivered involuntarily, suddenly feeling vulnerable, isolated and alone. Still in denial about how his own actions had led to his arrest, he dearly wished his father were still alive to help him.

Simon sat heavily on the bed, sliding his fingers through his hair, and resigned himself to his discomfort and growing hunger. The last 20 hours had flashed by so quickly with one shock quickly succeeded by another. He still couldn't fully grasp how he had managed to end up in a Miami police station on a murder charge, and was starting to appreciate fully the cost of not insisting on having his lawyer, Brad Tavistock, present during his interview with Tanner. The misplaced confidence that accompanied his arrogance had exposed his weaknesses, and now the police would undoubtedly probe more deeply into Elsa Bartelli's disappearance with the sole objective of linking him to her murder. His mind reeled for the tenth time that day, sifting through the details of the interview with Tanner and the explanation of his actions to Bridget in a desperate search for contradictions that might be exploited by the police. He had to be sure as he planned to use his explanation to Bridget as a brief for Tavistock. And for the tenth time that day, he also regretted not consulting Tavistock beforehand who would have offered advice on what questions to answer and more importantly, the ones to avoid. Before being whisked away by the NYPD and Tanner, Walsh had asked Bridget to get in touch with Tavistock and advise him of his arrest and imminent departure for Miami.

Bridget was a little bemused by the sudden turn of events, apparently showing no emotion as her husband was being taken away. She had wrestled privately with the prospect of having to come to terms with the possibility that her husband was a murderer, but she managed to maintain her composure by trying to convince herself that his arrest was merely speculative. It just allowed the MPD to engage in more detailed questioning before discounting him as a suspect. The thought of his arrest had never crossed her mind during her interview with Tanner.

Walsh reflected that the maid, Francesca, had seemed to show more distress at his arrest than Bridget. He wasn't sure whether Bridget thought him capable of murder or not and didn't really know whether he could rely on her support. If there was a trial and she decided not to appear, he knew her absence would send out the wrong signal to the jury, who might take it as a sign that she believed him to be guilty. He wondered if she already did.

Alone in his cell, Walsh had to face the stark reality of his circumstances and the grim possibility of going to trial for Elsa Bartelli's murder. He comforted himself by comparing his current situation with the night he had spent in a New Orleans jail, but his optimism was short-lived, remembering his father was no longer around to clean up after him. Seán Walsh had taken good care of the hooker his drunken son had beaten by arranging hospital treatment in one of the best clinics in the city. He had also handsomely paid off the madam of the brothel to work on the girl and make sure assault charges weren't brought against Simon at a later date. The New Orleans police commissioner deferred bringing an aggravated assault charge against Simon as a personal favor to his father.

Walsh had a lukewarm meal of beans, burned hamburger and runny eggs before settling down for the night. He ran the movie reel of events of that fateful, damned boat trip over and over in his brain, trying to find any angle that the police could use to try and pin a homicide charge on him. The more he thought about it, the more comforted he felt, and he assured himself it was unlikely that the police had any hard evidence against him. Finally, having convinced himself that his arrest was just a pathetic attempt by the police to get him to confess to murder, Walsh closed his eyes and went to sleep.

At 9 a.m. sharp the next morning, Brad Tavistock arrived at the prison. After going through security procedures, he was shown into the interview room. The lawyer gave Walsh a cursory nod as they sat down. Tavistock was not confident of his client's innocence, as he knew about Walsh's violent history and the extreme measures his father had taken to protect him. Eager to forego the pleasantries, he immediately began questioning him. Tavistock desperately wanted to get a better understanding of the facts behind the police files, and the stories he'd read. He needed to get a clear measure of the challenge ahead of him.

"Hello, Simon! I must say you have a rare talent for getting into difficult situations, and it always seems to involve ladies of ill repute."

Walsh leaned toward him. "I know it looks bad, Brad, but the police have nothing to go on. They're just flying a kite."

"I'm not so sure, Simon. In your interview with Detective Tanner, you said that you and Miss Bartelli had returned to the marina together. Evidence from a number of witnesses indicates that you lied to him. The prosecution will make capital out of that lie, and your defense will start with you having to establish your credibility to the jury. In addition to that, they have forensic evidence and detailed accounts of your movements that afternoon with and without Miss Bartelli. You were seen leaving the Ocean Drop Inn with the lady......."

"She was no lady, Brad. She knew exactly what she was doing, and sucked me into her little scheme before I even understood what was happening."

"You were later seen boarding your sports cruiser with the lady," Tavistock continued, ignoring Walsh's interruption, "but she was not with you when you returned. They've already analyzed hair and blood samples taken from your boat and the DNA matches perfectly with Miss Bartelli. The police have checked all possible places you could have put Miss Bartelli off your boat, and there is no record of you docking anywhere to do that! Finally, the police searched your house immediately after your arrest, and found your .45 automatic, which has been fired within the last two weeks."

Walsh's jaw dropped, he sat back and fixed his gaze on the wall behind Tavistock's head, his mind concentrating on the impact of his lawyer's assessment of the prosecution's evidence, and evaluating the damage.

"You've got to get me out of this, Brad," he blurted as if the gravity of his situation had suddenly hit him. His eyes darted back to meet those of his lawyer. "I don't care what it costs......whatever it takes, just...."

Tavistock cut him off, "Money's not going to help you, Simon. The police believe they've got sufficient evidence to charge you with homicide. Your best defense is to convince them of your innocence by starting to tell the truth. That is assuming you *are* innocent, of course."

"Don't tell me you think I killed her as well."

"Well, you're not giving me very much to work on, Simon," Tavistock breathed out and softened his tone. "Why don't you describe what happened so I can judge the best way to present your case and establish your credibility as an innocent man with the jury? I want to give them an alternative interpretation of the picture painted by the forensic evidence to the one the prosecution is going to put forward."

"Everything's more or less the way I said, except that we did have an argument. She panicked and ended up jumping off the boat. I searched for her but she didn't resurface. I guess she must have knocked herself unconscious when she hit the water."

"Blood stains were found on the deck; how did that happen?"

"OK, the argument turned physical when I found her with my wallet… she must have got hurt in the scuffle."

"Did you rape her or attempt to?"

"No. I didn't harm her in that way, Brad. You've got to believe me," Walsh pleaded sincerely.

"Good. That means that the police will not come up with any physical evidence from the boat indicating that you and she had intercourse. That would have given you a motive to kill her if you had taken her by force. For now, the only person who can tell the true story of what happened on that boat is you. I'm beginning to think you should take the stand, and convince the jury your version of events is the truth."

"It is, Brad. I wouldn't risk lying to you. I want you to believe in my innocence because it will make you more committed to getting me acquitted."

"It's not me you've got to convince, Simon. In future, don't say anything to the police or anybody else, for that matter, without my being beside you. They will want to interview you sometime today, but I want to prepare a statement for them to prevent their interview with you happening before we've had time to get your story straight." Tavistock was about to leave, but turned again to Walsh, and asked, "Why didn't you report the incident when you got back to shore?"

Walsh was stuck momentarily for an answer, but then decided to give the excuse he gave Bridget. "Given my past history, I was petrified because Bartelli's action was illogical and extreme. How could I explain it without giving the impression I tried to assault her?"

Tavistock still couldn't decide on his client's guilt or innocence. Truthfully, he didn't really care one way or the other, as he would do his best to protect Simon Walsh no matter how the case stacked up. He owed Seán that much. The media frenzy and consequent muckraking that would follow a conviction, and the inevitable slur it would put on Seán Walsh's good name had triggered his deep sense of loyalty to Seán in accepting Bridget Walsh's request to represent her husband. Normally, he wouldn't have given Simon Walsh the time of day, but he felt he had a duty to defend him for the sake of his dead father. Walsh's story was far from convincing, and Tavistock knew that he would need to go over it several times to make it sound plausible and he would also need to prepare Walsh for a grueling cross-examination.

When he got back to his office, he briefed his assistant, John Delaney, on the interview he'd had with Walsh, his uncertainty about their client's guilt and whether a murder had actually been committed. Despite their reservations, they were determined to do the best they could for their client, however both lawyers were convinced that after a review of the evidence during the arraignment hearing, the case would go to trial.

16:

BOSTON

With Walsh under arrest, the prosecution team were busy tying up all of the loose ends to make sure there would be no hiccups in court. Both Jack and Roland had been interviewed to get background on why Elsa was in Miami and to determine whether she drew a line on the things she would do in her act, or if she had her own sideline going with the customers of the Blue Cockatoo outside working hours. Jack confirmed that Elsa was in Miami alone because she had decided she needed a break and he was unable to drop everything at short notice due to work commitments. He said he wasn't worried because he knew of the arrangement with Julie to pick her up at the airport and felt chill-out time would help her as working at the Blue Cockatoo could get claustrophobic.

Initially, Bantry had called up Bannister to resume their acquaintance and asked if Elsa was a hooker in her own time and if there was any likelihood Walsh was telling the truth. Roland assured him that her relationship with patrons of the nightclub was strictly limited to dancing and that she didn't even do private lap-dancing sessions, which were very lucrative for the girls and sometimes led to 'private work'. He provided Bantry's team with the file he had on Elsa and some publicity photos. Some of the girls were also interviewed; they all confirmed Elsa only danced at the club and did not mix with the dancers or the customers outside working hours.

More recently their discussions eventually led to the probability of Walsh being prosecuted. Bantry told Bannister that the likelihood was that he would be prosecuted for second-degree murder, including the use of a firearm, and he would go through arraignment in the next few weeks.

Jack thought Elsa could be out of circulation for some time. The time between the arraignment hearing and the trial could be half a year depending on the court calendar. Elsa couldn't be expected to hibernate while in hiding and would need some means of identification. Jack knew Julie could drive, but didn't have a current driving license as she considered it pointless for anyone living in New York. Julie was persuaded to get a driving license which was then copied with a photograph of Elsa. Freddy Bartholomew, who had the reputation of being one of the best forgers in the business, made the copy.

Jack was getting worried about Elsa being seen in New York, and decided to rent a house in the Boston suburbs, where she could stay until Walsh had met their demands. She wasn't happy about moving out of Jack's apartment, but understood his concern, which made sense despite her becoming marooned. They had discussed a number of alternative locations, but Boston came out top because of its large population of more than 650,000, and its 200-mile distance from New York City. They hired a car for the journey, and paid for it in cash.

There was little conversation between them until after they had left the outskirts of the city. "Remind me why I have to go to Boston," Elsa said, pouting.

"Now that Walsh has been arrested, we can't take the chance of you being seen in New York," Jack replied patiently. "The trial will probably result in your picture being plastered all over the tabloids because of your link to New York, increasing the chance of you being seen." They had discussed the need for her to leave New York several times, and he was finding it difficult to control his impatience with her, although he understood her misery.

"How can I be seen out and about in New York when I've been a prisoner in your apartment for the last two weeks?"

"I know, honey, but we've got to be cautious. We've come too far with this thing to blow it away through carelessness."

"You only ever 'honey' me when you want me to do something that you know I won't like. I know you're being a shit when you call me 'honey'. Don't try to sugarcoat it."

"Listen, Elsa. If Walsh goes to prison, we are both going to make a lot of money; enough to set us up for life. We can do whatever we like and go wherever we want after that."

"I know you've told me often enough over the past couple of weeks, but he's not in prison yet! Is he? I don't know how long it will take, and there are no guarantees."

"It's a high-profile murder case now, and knowing how the Miami DA likes to stay the right side of the public, I think it'll be processed quickly. I spent enough time in homicide to know that!" Jack replied tetchily, and added, "Besides, the prosecution have built up a strong case against him, with a good chance of winning."

"How can you be sure of that? Besides, the MPD is handling the case, and they might do things differently there."

"I've got some contacts in the MPD. They tell me they have sufficient evidence to take the case to trial from the forensic evidence retrieved from Walsh's boat alone that has been strengthened by witness testimonies. The only weakness in their case is in not having physical evidence, but I felt providing them with that would be going a little far. They can find their own body; I want yours."

Elsa smiled for the first time on their journey, turning her head away to hide her amusement from Jack. Events in Miami and her subsequent confinement in Jack's apartment had been depressing, apart from odd moments with Jack when he wasn't working or absorbed with Walsh. Surprisingly, she had found that she was missing her nightly stints at the Blue Cockatoo. She had come to realize her work there had provided a rhythm and pace to her life, which had been lost over the previous few weeks. She was even missing the banter with the customers and the other girls, but most of all, not exercising the feeling of power she got while she was performing. There was no way of releasing the stored energy built up from her inactivity. Now all she had to look forward to was the distant prospect of Walsh going to jail and being holed up in Boston for God knows how long.

"The best thing we have going for us is that Walsh thinks that he really did kill you," said Jack, snapping Elsa out of her thoughts.

"I know, Jack. You're starting to get repetitive."

"I can't overstress the importance of it, because it means he will feel he has something to hide from his lawyer, the judge and jury, everybody......even his wife. The jury will see Walsh every day of the trial and will pick up on his body language long before gets his chance to testify. If he decides to go on the stand any hesitancy or contradiction between what he's saying and the image he's projecting will betray him as much as his words. Let's hope he feels confident enough to give evidence, then a good DA will get him tongue-tied and show him up for the liar he really is."

"OK, Jack. Let's assume Walsh goes to prison. What then?"

"After he goes to prison, we'll need to make an approach to him from the inside. That won't be too difficult. Roland and I have a number of potential contacts in Florida, both inmates and officers. It will need to be handled delicately, but our man will let Walsh know that you survived your ordeal in the water and that for the right price you'll come forward to clear him."

"But won't the police be suspicious about my not coming forward earlier, particularly during the trial?"

"There could be any number of reasons ranging from amnesia to finding a remote place of sanctuary to recuperate from the experience. The best reason could be fear of retribution from Walsh. You thought him to be a vindictive man with the money to pay for people that could have intimidated you, or who would seek some kind of revenge, making you too frightened to come forward. It won't be difficult to fabricate a story, but we can work out the details later. How does Canada sound?"

"Cold!" Elsa replied curtly.

"On second thought, it may be difficult to get you out of the country, because you would have to go on a false passport and that might be difficult to explain."

"I don't care what you do as long as I don't end up facing police charges when I return," said Elsa beginning to feel exasperated again.

"We can plan out the timeline, beginning with you going into hiding to escape the possibility of retribution. You return to New York when Walsh has been sentenced and is safely in prison. We have to convince the authorities you didn't have enough time to find out what was happening to him and intervene in his trial. After all, the trial is big news in Miami with day-to-day updates, whereas only the outcome will be reported in New York."

"I'm yesterday's news already," Elsa cut in.

Unperturbed by Elsa's interjection, and not picking up on her boredom with the conversation, he continued. "Alternatively, you could convince the police that you initially wanted revenge on hearing of Walsh's plight. That would be understandable, and may even add credibility to your story."

Jack's matter-of-fact, analytical way of explaining his reasoning always annoyed Elsa. In his machinations, he didn't stop to think about the strain a long-term stay in Boston would put on her or the effect on her whole way of life, which she was already missing. While he was going through the options of explaining her return to the police, Elsa became aware that she would end up doing time, just like Walsh.

"Do you think Walsh will readily accept your offer? He may decide to initiate his own investigation if he finds out I'm still alive," Elsa asked, wanting to change the subject.

"He'll have a strong incentive to accept. Let's just say his incarceration may be fraught with disagreements with other inmates or officers, and those will incentivize his need to get out of prison as quickly as possible."

"I don't want him to be hurt, no matter what he did to me," said Elsa, alarmed at the possibility of him being beaten up in prison. She had read about the brutality inside some institutions.

"Don't worry! He won't be seriously hurt; just made to feel a little uncomfortable. He'll be unaccustomed to the stark reality of living in a prison where the rules are so completely different from the outside world. After being the top dog in his world, he'll then be just another inmate trying to survive. It'll be difficult for him, no matter what I do."

"Yes, but he's rich, surely......"

"Money doesn't really count for anything inside," Jack interjected. "Respect from the other inmates is what really counts, and it's the strong and powerful in the criminal world that command the greatest respect. Some crime lords are just as influential when they're in prison as when they're on the outside, and they don't hesitate to use brute force to bend people to their will. Walsh won't have any credibility in prison because he's lived his life outside the criminal world, but they may humor, or even protect him, if he promises them money. I don't really know. All I do know is that it will be a massive culture shock for him, and that he'll have to tread very carefully until he finds out the lie of the land."

"I'm still worried that he'll be seriously hurt. Do you really think we're doing the right thing?" said Elsa, finding another reason to regret the venture they had begun.

"Nobody's going to hurt Walsh unless he gives them a good reason for it. He's just got to keep a low profile and make sure he doesn't annoy anybody," said Jack, amazed that Elsa could be compassionate after being shot and left for dead.

A sign for a diner appeared on the side of the highway, and driving toward it, Jack said, "Let's pull into that diner. All this talking is making me thirsty."

Elsa and Jack walked into the diner and sat at the table furthest from the door. "I can see why Roland is wary of you, Jack. You've got this whole thing planned out to the last detail. Roland and I are just spectators."

"Don't think that! We're a team, and we all need each other. We'll only be strong and stay strong if we have a mutual bond of trust between us. Roland is a control freak, and added to that, he's just nervous about losing the money he's already invested heavily in the scam. But that's not his major consideration."

"I know. The money isn't really what's important to him. Roland doesn't like to be a bit player; he likes to control things. Power gives him a buzz, so he's uncomfortable with you calling all the shots. Get him more involved, or just talk to him more; anything to reduce the tension that's beginning to build up between the two of you."

A waitress came over to their table to take an order. Jack broke their conversation and took two menus from the waitress and handed one to Elsa. Skimming through their menus they decided to order coffee and plain pancakes. The waitress took their order to the kitchen and quickly returned with cups and saucers, milk and a jug of coffee. She topped up the cups with coffee and promised the pancakes wouldn't be long in coming.

Jack took a sip of his drink and said, "Roland seems pleased enough with the way things are going and with me acting as go-between with Walsh through his wife Bridget. Roland's happy for me to take the reins because he doesn't want to get too involved with the business end, and he's covering his ass, just in case things don't go to plan."

"Why is his ass any more sensitive than ours? God knows he'll be making as much money as we do."

"Actually, he'll be taking slightly more than us, because he's funding the gig. I've agreed a 40-30-30 split with him taking the lion's share. Together we'll still be taking most of the pot, so I didn't see any reason to argue about his extra 10 percent.

"Well, so much for our being a team. Why wasn't I involved in the decision? It's my money as well as yours! You may have invested your time, Roland his money, but I've given up my life!"

At this point, the waitress returned to the table with their pancakes. She could hear the vehemence in Elsa's tone of voice as she was talking to Jack and that her face was flushed with emotion. "Are you alright?" she asked with obvious concern. Elsa nodded pulling a handkerchief from her handbag and wiping her nose. The waitress put Elsa's plate of pancakes down in front of her, saying, "I don't know what the problem is, honey, but believe me they're not worth the heartache." With that, she dropped Jack's plate of pancakes in front of him and turned on her heel. She came back quickly with the syrup and Jack was relieved he didn't end up having it poured into his lap.

"Obviously, you're not such a hit with all women. There are some situations that you just can't manage because, like it or not, someone will always get the wrong end of the stick," Elsa said, smiling and enjoying her small triumph. "Tell me more about you acting as a go-between with Walsh and his wife."

"By all accounts, she's a very cool customer and her relationship with her husband is not what you'd expect from a loving couple. In many ways, that will be an advantage because she won't be overemotional and won't let extraneous influences cloud her judgement. Besides, she needs the support of her husband to operate in her current role as company secretary at the NMP. Her husband's support is essential because she's an outsider who was brought into the company when she married Walsh. By all accounts, she's ambitious and has worked her way up in people's estimation in a very short space of time, so she's bound to appreciate the quick return of her husband, as it'll take pressure off her from other quarters. I'm assuming some directors will be calling for her head when he's convicted. If she can fend them off until Walsh is cleared, it will motivate her to ensure our transaction moves quickly."

"But why should she talk to you, and why won't she go straight to the police when she finds out the truth?"

"Whoever we get to put the squeeze on Walsh in prison will suggest he gets his wife to contact me to make arrangements for the handover of the money. To Bridget, my role will be that of the arbitrator between her and the people keeping you in hiding, rather than as one of the people trying to extort money from her. To do that, I'll need to convince her that I've been hired for the job and have no involvement in the scheme, or have any knowledge of your whereabouts. I'll tell her that I only agreed to take the job to help protect her as an innocent party. That way, she won't want to take the risk of going to the police and losing the chance to free her husband."

"I don't know, Jack; I think it's a long shot. It will take a lot to convince her that you're an honest Joe working in her best interests. It seems a risky proposition to me, because if she does go to the police, they'll quickly link you to me."

"The media weren't interested in me or our relationship. They had far more lurid things to report than your love life. I never gave an interview and my name was only briefly mentioned in the early reports. They won't connect my name to you."

"Why can't Roland be the go between?" Elsa asked.

"Roland has a much higher media profile than me, being the owner of the Blue Cockatoo and supplying photographs of you dancing at the club. The only alternative would be to bring someone else in, and you know that the more people who know what's going on, the greater the risk of Walsh or the police finding out. And it would reduce our payout."

"All you think about is the money. I hope it gets you everything you want at the end of the day, because it will be a massive disappointment to you if it doesn't."

"It's not just for me; it's for both of us. Don't you understand that having Walsh's money will mean that we'll never have to work again if we don't want to? You don't want to be dancing every night at the Blue Cockatoo for the next 10 years, do you?"

"I suppose not," Elsa replied. They got up from the table and Jack gave Elsa a quick peck on the cheek before they moved toward the exit. This little show of affection relieved some of the tension Elsa had been feeling since the start of the trip, and she began to relax a little.

As she was leaving the diner, Elsa turned toward the waitress who had served them, smiled and thanked her for her service. The waitress smiled back, wishing her a good onward journey. After Jack and Elsa had left the diner, she turned to a colleague, saying, "Haven't I always told you men just can't be trusted?"

17:

TRIAL BEGINS

The judge appointed to preside over Walsh's arraignment was Wesley Hyam, a man known to support women's rights and to have traditional moral values, abhorring the sleazy, free-and-easy sex culture of the big cities. He had worked the Florida circuit for 20 years, and was now close to retirement. On the basis of the evidence provided at the arraignment hearing, he recommended that Walsh be prosecuted for second-degree murder, but accepted Tavistock's proposal that a lesser charge of manslaughter could be considered if the jury could not agree to the murder charge. It was anticipated that the trial would not take longer than three weeks, and a date was scheduled in the court calendar.

The next six months prior to the trial passed quickly for Jack but very slowly for Elsa up in Boston. Jack could feel the tension building between them, and he persuaded Bannister to let Julie go and live with her to reduce her feeling of isolation. Reluctantly, Bannister agreed, but accepted Julie would relieve some of the tedium of her friend's exile and help the time pass more quickly. Walsh was released on bail, but he took an extended leave of absence from his company to pacify shareholders and the Board of Directors. He was in no mental state to resume his duties, never mind act as the executive officer of the company. The time passed slowly for both Walsh and Elsa, who were bored out of their minds, having to 'tread water' until the end of the trial. They were both impatient for the trial to begin so they could get on with their lives, but Walsh remained apprehensive of the outcome.

The trial process began with the qualification and swearing in of jurors. Hyam was determined to ensure that the jury would include a reasonable number of women to get an even balance and ensure the female perspective of the case was considered. The prosecution and defense teams had prepared profiles of the likely jurors following the initial qualification process. Tavistock had objected to one well-known feminist activist, but generally the process had gone reasonably smoothly with little sign of friction between the two lead lawyers, and Hyam hoped both men would continue to be objective during the actual trial.

The teams for the prosecution and the defense had worked frenetically up to the start of the trial examining and re-examining every bit of detail to be able to deal with any eventuality. Bantry saw himself as an athlete training for the big event, whereas Tavistock had a less romantic view of himself, imagining that he was the guardian of Seán Walsh's name and reputation. Both lead lawyers wanted to win the case on their terms. Bantry was relatively young and dynamic, hoping to astound the jury with his reasoning and rhetoric, whereas Tavistock expected to adopt a thorough but measured approach, appealing to the common sense of the jury.

The court usher announced the entrance of Judge Hyam to the courtroom, and everyone stood up. The trial had drawn a large crowd because of the revived media publicity preceding it. Most people had come to see in the flesh the characters they had been reading about. They would undoubtedly be disappointed when they realized there was nothing particularly different or spectacular about them, and attendances would progressively diminish as the trial progressed. Hyam entered the courtroom and took his seat. He was a big man who was not very mobile, even allowing for his advanced years, and he sat down heavily with more than a hint of relief. The court clerk then declared that everyone else should be seated. Hyam announced that proceedings were for the trial of Simon Walsh, accused of the murder of Elsa Bartelli, and confirmed the attendance of the defense and prosecution attorneys. He requested a plea from Simon Walsh, which was given as "Not guilty". Brushing his forehead, Hyam instructed the prosecution and defense attorneys to put forward their opening statements, beginning with the prosecution.

Hyam was known to give lawyers a free rein when addressing the jury, and Bantry stood up and walked over to the jurors trying to make eye contact with each and every one of them.

"Simon Walsh is a man used to getting what he wants," he began, "and when in difficulty, pulls out his checkbook. Consequently, he now believes everything and everyone has a price. This reasoning is applied to whatever he desires. It may be cars, yachts, diamonds or women. It makes no difference because to him these things are all 'commodities' to be purchased for his use."

Bantry noted indignant glances from some of the female jurors, which pleased him as it confirmed that they were already feeling a personal dislike for Walsh because of his reported attitude to women.

"But women, of course, are not commodities, not that recent history can show Walsh making such a subtle distinction. On June 16 last, he took a beautiful young woman, Elsa Bartelli, on board his sports cruiser for what should have been a pleasant boat trip on a lovely, sunny afternoon."

Bantry knew that the jurors would probably have read about Elsa's disappearance, and no doubt, formed their own opinions on the circumstances leading to her afternoon with Walsh and the underlying reason for her to agree to go on his boat. If they had taken any interest in the case, they would also know of her colorful background and that she was an exotic dancer. Bantry wanted to portray Elsa in the best possible light, while at the same time destroying any last vestiges of sympathy the jury might still have for Walsh.

"Elsa was on vacation and probably excited at going out with Walsh on his private boat, which was a far cry from the social circles she usually mixed in at home in New York. But Walsh had an ulterior motive for asking Elsa to spend the afternoon with him," said Bantry, glancing contemptuously sideways at Walsh. Pointing directly at the accused man, he continued, "This man took the unfortunate young woman on his boat with the intention of compromising her to gratify his own base lust. But she was not a person to be intimidated by Walsh or anyone else for that matter. She stood up to him and a scuffle ensued with him finally shooting her. After dumping her body at sea, he returned to the harbor without a trace of remorse or guilt for the crime he had just committed. His lack of remorse is clearly illustrated by the casual telephone call he made to his wife only hours after shooting Elsa and leaving her to perish in the sea!"

Walsh shifted uncomfortably in his seat and chatted to his attorney as if picking errors in Bantry's opening statement or explaining the actual events on the day. Bantry noted that most of the jurors had now focused their attention on Walsh and were trying to determine whether he would be capable of cold-blooded murder. Four of the jury were women, who would instinctively sympathize with Elsa's plight, particularly if they themselves had experienced the unwelcome advances of strangers, or been placed in compromising situations. Bantry had to remain diligent throughout the trial to ensure that these women did not lose their bond with Elsa by the protracted dissection and analysis of her lifestyle.

"You will hear that Elsa was an exotic dancer in a New York nightclub and used her body for the titillation of men. This aspect of her life has been given a lot of coverage by the media, but don't let their tawdry speculation about Elsa influence your judgement of her without first hearing the facts. Yes, she was an exotic dancer and she was very popular with the customers of the Blue Cockatoo. By all reliable reports she was capable of taking care of herself with anyone who became too friendly, but that was because she was working in a controlled environment and not isolated on her own somewhere out at sea."

"The fact that she bared her body to strangers does not mean that she was a person of low morals, or that she deserved to be treated any differently from any other woman. Every woman has the right to say no to an unwanted sexual advance, and no woman should be subjected to the crudity Walsh tried to impose on Elsa. Remember that she was not in her normal environment where she was prepared for lewd advances, so the attack from Walsh was unexpected. Yes, she showed a lack of caution and judgement by going out with him after knowing him for such a short time, but he is overtly rich and influential, and she could be excused for not anticipating she would be compromised in such a way."

"When questioned by police, Walsh lied to them, saying that he had brought Elsa back to the marina. It was only after his arrest that he admitted they had fought, and Elsa had jumped overboard. Ladies and gentlemen, they were a mile out at sea. Does that really seem credible?" Bantry once again turned to Walsh. "I will show you that this man murdered Elsa Bartelli in cold blood, and believed that his wealth and social position would place him above the law. But he now finds himself in court charged with her murder, and I want to make sure we provide justice for Elsa."

"Thank you, Mr. Bantry. Your turn, Mr. Tavistock," said Judge Hyam with a resigned almost bored tone of voice. He was used to the theatrics of counsels at this stage in the proceedings, which were generally unimaginative and strangely predictable.

Tavistock stood up, and smiled at the jury.

"Mr. Bantry would have you believe that Miss Bartelli was an innocent abroad caught up in the clutches of an evil man and unable to defend herself against his lascivious advances. Take off your rose-colored spectacles. She was a woman who gyrated semi-naked in front of men. She has been described as an exotic dancer; that is a little misleading as that implies that there is some artistic merit in her dancing. The real term is lap dancer; her job was to thrust every private part of her body into the faces of men who treat them as fantasy figures. These men reciprocate by attaching money to any brief item of clothing the lap dancer may be wearing. Believe me Elsa Bartelli was hardly an innocent."

"Although I speak of Miss Bartelli in the past tense, a body has not been produced to confirm her death. It is possible that she could have swum back to land, and if she did, I can't explain why she hasn't come forward. If she is dead, she brought it upon herself by trying to steal my client's money and credit cards, and then making an irrational attempt to escape when she was caught. She was the perpetrator of a crime, and my client was the victim."

He did everything he could to get her back onto the boat, drawing the line at jumping into the sea after her. If she had climbed back onto the boat while he was searching for her, she could have left him to drown. He searched for her until the light started to fade, and after such a long time, feared she had drowned."

From the expressions on some of the juror's faces, Tavistock could see that they were questioning the credibility of Walsh's attempts to rescue Elsa. Tavistock himself had wrestled with Walsh's story and whether anyone would risk their life to avoid a minor theft or soliciting charge. Tavistock concluded that the only chance Walsh had of beating the murder charge would be to convince the jury he had no hidden agenda to have sex with Elsa, and that would be the biggest challenge.

"The prosecution has put together a flimsy circumstantial case filled with emotive arguments. I will steer you through the fog they have created and show that there aren't any hard facts to support their case. Most significantly there is no physical evidence. Her body has not been found, and the occurrence of a crime is not substantiated. Their whole case is based on circumstantial evidence, which is open to interpretation. Members of the jury, I will ask you to find Simon Walsh innocent of these preposterous charges."

Walsh turned around to smile at Bridget, who was sitting in the first row of the spectators' area. She had reluctantly decided to attend the trial because she understood that she had to be supportive of her husband to create the right impression for the judge, the jury, the media and the Board of Directors of the NMP.

Six rows behind her sat Jack Cates, on the opposite side of the courtroom. He had been observing Bridget during the opening remarks of the prosecution and defense attorneys, looking for any reaction to their statements, which could give him an insight into her feelings toward her husband and her mental state during this ordeal. Despite the confidence he had in the ultimate success of the prosecution, Jack recognized that his dealings with Bridget after her husband's conviction would be difficult, and the success of the plan hinged on getting her to believe he was working in the best interests of Simon.

With her blond hair and Scandinavian features, the woman was undoubtedly attractive, but in a less earthy way than Elsa's Italian ancestry. She appeared aloof and disinterested in the proceedings. The uninformed observer would never have guessed that she had a personal interest in the trial, never mind that her husband was fighting a murder charge. Jack remembered his father's expression to describe people with her demeanor. He would say that they built a wall around themselves by going about with their nose in the air, trying to avoid eye contact with everyone. Although he found Walsh's attitude to women abhorrent, he wondered if his cold and loveless marriage was a possible factor in forming his attitude toward them.

After a recess for lunch, the first prosecution witness was put on the stand. It was Jerry, the barman from the Ocean Drop Inn. As the joint owner of the bar, Jerry was well respected and more importantly, trusted. He confirmed that Elsa and Walsh had left the bar together, and that Walsh was clearly taken with her. Jerry also confirmed that when vacationing in Miami, Walsh often used to meet women in his bar and take them out on his boat. The implication that Walsh would use his boat as a means to seduce women was clear. When questioned by Tavistock, Jerry stated that Elsa had been in the bar every day of that week, drinking several vodka tonics on each occasion. To Tavistock's delight, Jerry ventured his opinion that Elsa was a hooker waiting for a high roller. Despite Bantry's objection and the striking of the remark from the record, the jury would remember what Jerry had said, and place another black mark against Elsa.

Other witnesses followed Jerry to confirm the movements of Elsa and Walsh that fateful afternoon, but the next influential witness to take the stand was the forensic examiner of the Miami Police Department. He stated that the DNA testing of blood samples taken from the deck of Walsh's boat matched the DNA of hair samples taken from Elsa's hair brush. He also found hair samples on the boat that matched her DNA. His final damning bit of evidence was that forensic tests on Walsh's gun confirmed it had been fired on the day of Elsa's disappearance.

The prosecution presented their case during the first week of the trial, and Bantry felt he had done a reasonable job. He had painted a clear picture of the events that had taken place on Walsh's boat and was ably supported by forensic evidence and witness statements. The only person able to challenge the story he had presented to the court was Walsh himself. If Walsh took the stand, he would give Bantry the opportunity to expose the deep flaws in his version of events. Jerry's comments about Elsa being a hooker had tainted the jury's image of her, but on balance, he thought he was ahead of the game.

On the other side of the courtroom the defense attorney was anxious. Tavistock knew he had a mountain to climb to prove Walsh's innocence, and already sensed several members of the jury were already leaning toward the prosecution's version of events. Although the prosecution had proven that Elsa had been on Walsh's boat, and that a fight had taken place, the circumstances of her disappearance were still open to interpretation. He would have to convince Walsh to take the stand and persuade the jury he had not done anything to make her want to jump off his boat. It was risky because his client would have to weather the cross-examination by Bantry, and if he was guilty and unable to think quickly, he could incriminate himself.

18:

SHAKEDOWN

Jack was having a quiet drink before going to his hotel when he heard someone behind him say, "It's a small world isn't it, Mr. Cates?" Jack spun on his bar stool to face the man speaking to him. "It's me, Al Ferrino, the guy in charge of the motorboats at the marina. Don't you remember me?"

"Oh, yes. Hi, Al! I'm sorry for not recognizing you straight away but you caught me unaware," Jack replied.

"That's OK, Jack. I recognized you right off in court. You know they didn't call me as a witness, but my statement was read out. How do you think it's going?"

"Who knows? It seems clear to me that he killed the girl, but there's still a long way to go before the jury decide on his guilt. I'll have a better idea after I've heard the defense."

"The girl was on the boat, but isn't it funny they never found a body? Still the tide may have dragged her out to sea.... and then there are sharks. By the way, I got your second payment of $5,000. Thanks."

"That's OK, Al. You earned it by making sure that the people who were able to bring Walsh to justice went to the police. It was very public spirited of you to do that." The man was angling for something and also starting to get on Jack's nerves. The last thing he wanted to do was discuss the trial with Al in a bar within spitting distance of the courthouse. The attendant had been paid handsomely for his efforts, but it was obvious he was going to try and squeeze Jack for more money.

"I still say it's strange that a body wasn't found, isn't it?" Al repeated and took another swig from his bottle of beer. "Was that girl, Elsa Bartelli, connected to you in any way?"

"Well, you're sure are full of questions today, Al. Last time we met, I could barely get a word out of you."

"Well, that's because I'm involved in the trial in a small way and I've really taken an interest in the case. Most people seem to think that Walsh will be convicted. What about you?"

"My opinion won't change anything that happens in the court, so it's irrelevant."

"Not at all, Jack. The defense doesn't know where the girl's body is, but you do, don't you?"

Jack's body stiffened and he leaned forward until his face was a couple of inches away from Al. "I hope you and me are not going to fall out over a technicality like the resting place of this girl's body. Don't get clever with me, and above all, don't try to threaten me."

Al was visibly shaken by Jack's threatening posture and tone, but he hadn't come this far to stop now. "I know that Elsa is alive and living in Boston. How can a public-spirited guy like me keep that information quiet?" he countered.

"Listen carefully. You've been paid well for your help. Now, don't rock the boat and quit while you're ahead," Jack answered coldly.

Al's earlier bravado was quickly dissipating, but he decided to carry on in spite of his natural instinct to turn tail and run. "Look, Jack. You paid me and that's fine, but it got me wondering. You gave me $10,000 for doing next to nothing, so what's in it for you? I don't know what you're planning, but it must be plenty."

"You're batting out of your league, Al. If you stick your head above the ramparts then it's likely to get shot off. I'm saying this for your own good, you're moving into dangerous territory."

"Don't fuck with me Jack because I know I'm holding the trump card. I want more money, not a lot, just enough to buy myself a nice place and retire. You know a man in my position has got to push this thing for all its worth," said Al regaining his bravado.

"How much more do you want?"

"150 grand, or the police get a message about Elsa's whereabouts. I know you could move her, but she's bound to leave a trail no matter how careful you are, and my message will give the police sufficient incentive to try and follow the trail. It would certainly blow a hole in the prosecution's case and could stall the trial."

"That's more money than I can get together before the end of the trial," Jack replied calmly. "I'll be in the court until it's finished, so you'll have to wait until then."

Al thought the trial would only go on for another three or four days, and although waiting for the money could reduce his leverage, he felt he had the whip hand in any future negotiations. The initial newspaper reports on Elsa's disappearance mentioned her boyfriend Jack Cates, a New York private detective, who he guessed was the man who gave him $10,000. Then, on hearing Walsh had been arrested, Al took a few days' vacation, flew to New York and tailed Jack on the hunch he could find out a bit more on what he was planning.

It was a long shot, but luckily, within the first three days of sitting outside Jack's apartment block, Jack came out with Elsa and got into their car. He followed them to Boston, and to the address where Elsa was to sit in hiding. Jack's plan obviously hinged on the disappearance of Elsa and the conviction of Walsh. Al didn't care about the reasons behind Jack's deception, but knew it must involve a lot of money and he had more than enough to blackmail Jack into paying up.

"That's fine, but please don't get smart, Jack. I'll give you two days after the trial to get the money together, otherwise I go to the cops."

"You don't give a guy a lot of choices, do you, Al?"

"What I'm asking for is probably a pimple on the stash that you'll be making. Walsh must be worth millions. Don't forget, Jack, it's the money or the cops." With that, Al finished his beer and left without saying another word.

Jack pondered the ultimatum given him by Al. He was surprised the little man had worked up sufficient courage to confront him, and he smiled to himself at the thought of being intimidated by a short, overweight, middle-aged boat attendant. He was still lost in his thoughts when a lithe, blond woman took the stool vacated by Al. Jack turned to look at her, but didn't really see her as he was still preoccupied with Al's threat.

"Is your friend coming back?" she asked after giving her order to the barman.

"No. It's OK. He's gone and won't be back."

Jack smiled again, knowing Al would be back with his hand out. Although he was amused by the situation, Jack knew it would have to be handled carefully. If Roland found out about Al's threat to go to the police all hell would break loose, and Jack was sure that Roland wouldn't handle the matter delicately, or see the funny side of the situation.

"Well, you're a happy man, or are you just drunk?" the blond asked.

"I'm not drunk now, but hopefully that situation will change before the end of the night," Jack replied.

"Well, if you're on your own, so am I…. Maybe we could spend some time together."

Jack looked quizzically at the woman looking for an angle.

"There's no need to look at me like that, man. I'm not a hooker. It's just that Miami can be flat when you're on your own."

"I'm sorry, sugar. It's just I have a suspicious mind. I'm an ex-cop. Let me make up for my bad manners by getting you a drink."

"I only ordered this one a minute ago."

"Hell! Once we get started it could be a very long night," said Jack, lifting his glass to hers.

Lying in bed in his hotel room in the early hours of the morning, Jack lit a cigarette, drew in deeply, and exhaled slowly. He turned to look at the blond lying next to him. She was asleep, apparently spent after frenetic bouts of drinking and lovemaking. Jack had been celibate since Elsa went to Boston and he had forgotten just how badly he needed sex. He felt a little guilty about being unfaithful to Elsa, but that was not what was gnawing away in the back of his mind; he was still thinking about how he could dissuade Al from carrying out his threat. He didn't like using violence to get what he wanted, but resigned himself to the fact that he would have to give the little man a severe beating to make him understand he shouldn't upset the big boys. Some shakedown!

19:

WALSH TAKES THE STAND

Tavistock spent hours talking to Walsh, trying to convince him of the need to take the stand and tell the jury his side of the story. The attorney believed it was the only way his client could credibly present himself as the victim of a crime, rather than as a murderer. It was risky, as Walsh would have to be clear and coherent, and project an image of decency to convince the jury of his honesty. At the same time, he'd have to think quickly to be able to respond to the questions fired at him under cross-examination. Tavistock had spent many more hours schooling him thoroughly, and they had played out every possible line of questioning that could be thrown at him.

The lead defense attorney was nervous but confident that he had given his client the armory to defend himself adequately under cross-examination, and when Walsh was called to the stand, he strode across the courtroom confidently to take the oath.

"What is your name?" Tavistock opened after Walsh had been sworn in.

"Simon Walsh."

And what is your normal place of residence?"

"Suite 5, Manhattan Towers."

"That's a very select address, Mr. Walsh. You must be a very rich man."

"I am the chief executive of a major international insurance and banking company, and both my wife and I are on the main board of directors. Our combined income puts us in the Top 5 percent of U.S. joint-income earners."

Tavistock whistled. "You're a very privileged man, Mr. Walsh. It's a bit strange that you should put your position and reputation at risk by getting into a fight with a woman of the streets."

"Objection, Your Honor!" Bantry interjected. "The defense counsel is implying that Elsa Bartelli was a prostitute, and with such innuendo, he is prejudicing the juror's opinion of her and her reasons for meeting with Walsh on the fateful afternoon of her disappearance,"

"Objection sustained. Mr. Tavistock will you please stick to the facts and not allow your or anybody else's personal opinions to creep into the evidence," Judge Hyam scolded him.

Tavistock nodded apologetically. "Are you in the habit of seeking out the company of prostitutes? This is not a reference to Miss Bartelli, Your Honor."

Walsh had been warned by his attorney that this line of questioning would be introduced early in his testimony, explaining that it would be better to bring it out in the open rather than let the prosecution score points by revealing it later. "I won't deny that I've been with prostitutes and that I enjoy their company when I'm either on business or vacationing alone."

"Does your wife know of your relationship with these women?" Tavistock asked.

"Well, if she didn't, she does now," said Walsh, looking toward his wife in the courtroom. "These relationships mean nothing and are just one-night stands. I've always figured that it was better to satisfy my sexual needs that way than to betray my wife emotionally by getting involved in a complex relationship that could end up hurting her."

"Have you spoken to your wife recently about these liaisons?"

"Yes, we had a long talk before my arrest. In the past, she never questioned my behavior, provided I acted with discretion. This case has blown open my private life for everyone to pick over and make judgements on the kind of person I am. It has certainly shown me that I've been playing with fire all of these years, and I've been fortunate not to have found myself in a similar situation before this. I love my wife and don't want to risk hurting her anymore."

Bantry bristled at the sentiment gushing from Walsh, knowing of Rita Alonso's fate and also knowing he would not be able to present the facts of her case to the jury.

"I have noticed that your wife has attended the trial every day and obviously supports you fully," Tavistock commented.

"Yes, she has been very supportive, and in response, I've promised to remain faithful to her from now on."

"I know you will," Jack thought, "because you'll be in prison."

He was thankful that Elsa was in Boston and couldn't hear what was being said about her, because so far, the impression given to the jury was far from flattering.

"Let me take you back to June 16 last when you met Elsa Bartelli and took her on a boat trip. Had you and she previously met?"

"No, we hadn't. I went to the Ocean Drop Inn for a drink while my boat was being serviced, and I saw her sitting at the bar. There were no other people in the bar, except for an old couple sitting in the corner, and we started talking. There was no sexual intent on my part. I was only being friendly."

"Why did you end up taking her out on your boat?"

"She told me she was on vacation visiting her sister. Her sister was working that day, so she was using up time in the bar. It was the last day of her vacation, so I thought a private boat trip would help end her vacation on a high note."

"How did she introduce herself?"

She said her name was Lisa Millarno, so when the police started to question me about Elsa Bartelli, I didn't have a clue who they were talking about. When I was shown her picture, I recognized her, but started to worry what I was getting into."

"What do you mean?"

"I had no idea why I was being questioned. I know prostitution is illegal in Florida, so I worried about being charged for procuring sex. That wasn't my intention on this occasion. I just thought we could share a nice afternoon together. Of course, I know now that she was hustling me, and a relaxing afternoon in the sun wasn't what she was after."

"Why do you say that?"

"She may have been a hooker, but she wasn't like any hooker I've ever met before. Not that I go with street walkers, you understand. She was refined, and smartly dressed in designer clothes, and spoke in an educated way. I mean she had a breadth to her conversation that you wouldn't normally expect from a hooker. I don't mean that in a disrespectful way, but normally it's straight down to business with these girls after they've been paid."

"Objection, Your Honor!" Bantry cut in.

"I know, Mr. Bantry. Tell me, Mr. Tavistock, where are you going with this line of questioning?" Hyam responded.

"Elsa Bartelli didn't look or behave like a prostitute when my client first met her, therefore, he innocently took her out in his boat not expecting that she would try to seduce him. My cross-examination of Mr. Walsh will show you that Miss Bartelli's actions on his boat confirm our assumption that she was indeed a prostitute, and had sought out my client to compromise him, and extort or steal money from him."

"Very well, Mr. Tavistock, but remember what I said before about sticking to the facts."

"What happened when you got out of the harbor," Tavistock continued.

"We went out to the reef and dropped anchor. I had taken some spirits out with us and we both sat down for a drink, and started to talk about this and that, just getting to know one another. She eventually commented on how hot the sun was and would I mind if she took off her top. After her top, she

150

removed her shorts, and ended up in her underwear, then lay on the deck sunbathing."

"Did she encourage you in any way to lie down with her?"

"Not at first, but the sight of her was very tempting and I suppose, despite my earlier intentions, I couldn't help myself."

"Who made the first sexual advance?" Tavistock asked.

"To be honest, it's a little difficult to say. All I know is that we ended up kissing, then started caressing each other. I had been exercising a lot of restraint up to that point. After all, she had a beautiful body, and most of it was on display."

"Did she try and resist you at any time?"

"No. As my kissing and fondling became more intimate, she asked if I had protection. I went below deck to the bathroom to try and find a condom."

"Did you offer her money for sex?"

"No, that was the last thing on my mind. By this time, I couldn't think straight, and I just wanted to get my hands on a rubber as quickly as possible. I found what I wanted easily, but when I came back on deck, she was stuffing money and credit cards from my wallet into her handbag. I grabbed my wallet and took her handbag from her to check what she was trying to steal. After putting my things back into my wallet, I threw her handbag at her and told her to get dressed."

"How did she act after you discovered what she was trying to do?"

"She did nothing at first. If anything, she acted a little coquettish, as if it were all a game. I told her I was going to report her to the police when we returned to the marina and then she started to cry. She got very apologetic, begging me not to go to the police and that she would do anything if I didn't report her. By this time, I was completely sick of her antics and told her there was nothing she could do that would change my mind. Then she went berserk. She ran at me trying to scratch my face. I grabbed her wrists holding her at arm's length. She was trying to kick and bite me and eventually broke free of my grasp. Then she ran to the side of the boat and jumped overboard."

"Did you try and get her back onto the boat?"

"Of course, I did. I immediately went to the side of the boat to see what had happened to her. I couldn't see her in the water and didn't know if she had resurfaced. I shouted repeatedly but got no answer. I was worried about going in after her in case she got back on the boat while I was still in the water. Instead, I circled the area to try and find her, but without any luck."

"Did you kill Elsa Bartelli?" Tavistock asked directly, suddenly raising his voice a few decibels to emphasize his words.

"No, sir," Walsh responded steadfastly, slightly taken aback by his attorney's sudden change of tone, even though the pair had rehearsed this part of his testimony many times.

"Why didn't you report her disappearance to the coastguard?"

"I was shaken by the experience, and initially, couldn't think straight. I was scared that if anything had happened to her I would be accused of manslaughter or murder. I figured that if she was a good swimmer, she could have made it back to shore, and if she wasn't, she would be dead before the coastguard arrived anyway. I know that sounds cold-blooded but I was panicking and as I said it was difficult to think straight at the time."

Tavistock continued to elicit the well-rehearsed testimony from Walsh, ending with his client's expression of deep regret at what had happened. The jury seemed sympathetic at times, especially when he referred to the personal suffering he continued to endure in trying to live with the guilt of Elsa's possible death. Tavistock knew the battle wasn't over, and would only be happy if the jury remained sympathetic after Bantry's cross-examination.

Roland Bannister flew down to Miami when he heard Walsh was about to take the stand. There had already been suggestions that Elsa was a hooker, and he was sure these would be reinforced by Walsh's testimony. Elsa would be mortified to know that she was being portrayed as a cheap whore willing to peddle her body for money. It had been a long time since a case as juicy as this had been heard in Miami, and the television and press were making the most of their coverage of the trial. They weren't really concerned with the rights and wrongs of the case, just in sensationalizing Walsh's testimony to satisfy the public's appetite for sleazy drama. Bannister had played his part by furnishing them with a range of still photographs of Elsa in action, which he justified to Jack as being publicity for the Blue Cockatoo, as at the end of the trial, the story would probably be revisited by the national press.

Bannister and Jack were sitting together in one of the bars near the courtroom at the end of the first day of Walsh's testimony. They were both loath to agree that Walsh had done well on the stand and had probably raised his standing with the jury. It had been a credible performance with just the right amount of naive innocence, remorse and demonstration of affection for his wife. Both men were unconcerned about how the trial was going to finish, and they had every confidence that Bantry would expose Walsh for his true self. The defendant had to have at least one good day in court.

"Do you think Bantry will be able to tarnish the saintly image Walsh created for himself today?" Jack asked.

"I'm sure he will, but I don't know how deeply he can wound Walsh as far as Elsa is concerned, because everyone's convinced, she was hustling Walsh, and let's be honest, she was in fact doing the next best thing!"

Jack felt affronted by Bannister's statement.

"How can you talk about Elsa like that? You know she had more respect for herself than to act like some of the other girls at the club."

"You put her on show, Jack, for men to ogle."

"So do you."

"No, it's different at the club. Everyone knows what they're getting and respects the rules, and Elsa can keep her distance."

Jack felt defeated by Bannister's observation, as he had already searched his soul and admitted to himself that he had exploited Elsa, and what happened with Walsh was down to him.

Bannister continued, "He certainly gave a good performance today, and almost had me wanting to acquit him, and I know the truth! Don't worry. He won't have read the script before his session with Bantry. There'll be too many twists and turns in Bantry's line of questioning for him to cope with and no pat answers that he can churn out. I suppose it all depends on how well he can think on his feet."

Jack caught the eye of the barman and ordered a Napoleon Brandy for Bannister and got himself a Bud. "It may be a little premature for a celebration, but let's drink to a good outcome," said Jack.

The two men settled down with their drinks, silent for the moment and enjoying one of the simple pleasures of life. The silence was broken by the sound of Jack's cell phone. He pulled the phone from his inside pocket to answer the call. Bannister listened casually to the call from a man called Al.

"I thought we had agreed on the way ahead, Al, and that you should be patient...

...Yes, the trial is going well but it's still too soon to predict the outcome.........

.... If Walsh is convicted, he'll get what he deserves............

.... Don't bring Elsa into this again

...............Look. We can't talk about this over the phone. We'll have to meet..........

..................After the trial

Jack switched off his cell phone and put it into his pocket, returning to his drink, visibly irritated. Hearing Jack's side of the conversation, Bannister suspected he was trying to hide something, and it was obviously about the trial and Elsa. He caught Jack's attention, staring at him intensely and asking, "Is this something I should know about? Your phone call seemed to concern Elsa and Walsh, and your deal with some anonymous caller."

"Nobody important, Roland; just someone I'm having a little difficulty with at the moment. Don't worry. I've got it under control," Jack answered, trying to play down the importance of the call.

"Don't give me that, Jack! I heard you mention Elsa's name, so what was it all about?"

Reluctantly, Jack told Roland about Al's attempt to blackmail him for more money. "It was Al Ferrino from the marina — the guy who runs the motorboat concession. He knows Elsa's alive because he saw her with me when I returned the hire boat I used to follow Walsh. He says he wants $150,000, or he goes to the police. I've put him off until the end of the trial, which will give me time to scare him enough to forget about demanding any more money."

"The man is being a little too greedy, Jack. He got an easy ten grand for doing very little, and now he has the gall to ask for more! If we don't nip this in the bud, the jerk will always put his hand out whenever he needs something, and we'll never get rid of him. He's a loose cannon, and we don't know who he could be talking to."

"Don't blow it up out of proportion, Roland! The guy's a mouse. I'm surprised he even had the bottle to try and blackmail me. I'll make it clear that if he tries to cross us, he'll get seriously hurt."

"Now who's being dramatic? Look. I think you're taking this thing too lightly. This Al sounds unreliable and unpredictable, so putting the fear of God into him may not stop him going to the cops. After you've scared the life out of him, he'll go home, and in time he'll feel safe. It's then he'll either come back for the money, or blab to the cops. Besides, he can sink us either by design or just by blabbing one night when he's had a little too much to drink. He's looking at the biggest pay day of his life, so you can't expect him to roll over on your say so. Listen to me. We've got to handle this situation and do it quickly."

"OK, Roland, but he won't do anything until after the trial. He said he'd give me a few days after the verdict comes in to find his money."

"Well, he's certainly got nerve, I'll give him that," said Bannister. "Let's hope he doesn't live to regret it."

Roland Bannister decided to fly back to New York that evening, planning to get back to the Blue Cockatoo around midnight, just when the night wouldn't be kicking into top gear. He couldn't stay for Bantry's cross-examination and knew he'd get the full story from Jack and Bantry after the event.

Business was as good as ever at the club, but Roland knew his patrons would quickly go elsewhere if he didn't maintain his high standards. After Elsa's disappearance there was a slight fall in receipts, but takings returned to normal within a few months. Fortunately, moral degenerates can be a fickle bunch.

Bannister was less happy about the way Jack was handling Al Ferrino. He was amazed that his partner didn't seem concerned over the risk of the guy wrecking their plans. In contrast, Roland couldn't relax, knowing the damage the blackmailer could do on a whim. By the time his plane had arrived in New York, Bannister had decided to deal with the Al Ferrino situation himself, with Lou and Frank handling the details.

20:

DEEPER CRACKS

Jack stayed in the bar after Roland had left for the airport, and sat drinking another Bud while he was trying to decide on the best way of dealing with Al Ferrino. The poor guy didn't have a clue about the people he was trying to blackmail. If he understood the undercurrents of the cesspool he was dipping his toe into, he would never have approached Jack in the first place. He wondered how the little man had found out that Elsa was living in Boston. Al must have followed him on one of his trips to see her. Al was an amateur and was out of his depth. A professional would have mentioned the fact that he had registered a letter or some other document with his solicitor, detailing his side of the story and naming the people involved, as insurance for his own protection. Yes, an amateur; it'd be easy to show him the folly of trying to extort money from him without having to lean on him too hard.

While Jack was lost in thought, a woman came and sat at the opposite side of the table. She had a shock of platinum hair, partially covered by a chiffon headscarf that was tied under her chin. Although it was early evening, she was wearing sunglasses and was incongruously wrapped up in a white raincoat. It was hard to see her face, but her overall appearance was conspicuous in its absurdity, and reminded Jack of every femme fatale in every B movie he had ever seen when he was young.

"Do you mind if I sit here?" the woman asked in a light, breathy voice reminiscent of Marilyn Monroe.

Jack nodded, avoiding eye contact for fear of laughing out loud.

"I'm from out of town and I just want to know where a girl can get some action," she added, lowering her voice as if she were talking about a confidence between the two of them.

Jack's head whipped up to see the woman laughing at him. She lowered her sunglasses enough for him to see that it was Elsa. Without saying a word, he stood up, went around to the other side of the table, helped Elsa out of her seat, and the two walked out of the bar.

"You're coming down here was not one of your better ideas," said Jack as he drove to his hotel. "And besides, why wear something like that platinum wig and raincoat that will only attract attention to you," he added taking another look at her disguise. "Your whole appearance is ridiculous. You look like the caricature of a 1960s blond bombshell."

"I was missing you and I only dressed up like this to give you a bit of a laugh. I guess I shouldn't have bothered, should I?" Elsa replied dejectedly. "Look. It's OK for you and Roland up to your necks in Walsh's trial, but I'm holed up in a house on the outskirts of Boston and it's very boring. It's very difficult putting your life on hold while watching the rest of the world go by."

Jack was more than a little sympathetic to Elsa's situation and had seen a steady downturn in her morale over the time she had been living in Boston. He had tried to visit her as often as possible, but he still had to give the outward appearance of going about his day-to-day business to avoid attracting attention to himself. There had been other things like the memorial service he had arranged in her local church and commiserating with her friends.

The false sentiment was particularly difficult with people like Gus and Jean who took Elsa's disappearance very hard. They realized that Elsa had misled them by saying she was working in a dance troupe, but didn't think any the worse of her for working in the Blue Cockatoo. They didn't need labels to know she was a decent girl.

When they arrived at his hotel, Jack arranged for dinner and two bottles of wine to be sent to his room. Elsa wasn't pleased, "Do you think I've come all the way down to Miami to spend another night in a fucking hotel room?"

"I'd like to take you somewhere nice, Elsa, but if you're spotted, everything goes down the pan."

"There must be somewhere we can go with a little atmosphere."

"It's too risky. There's already someone here who knows that you're not dead."

"Who?" Elsa asked, suddenly feeling the wind knocked out of her sail.

"The motorboat attendant, Al Ferrino. He must have seen you getting out of the boat when we returned to the marina. He doesn't know what's behind our deception, but he's smart enough to figure out it's connected with Walsh's trial, and is asking for 150 grand."

"Does Roland know?"

"Yeah. He was with me at the bar when Al rang earlier, so I had to tell him what was going on. He thinks we should sort Al out straight away and I've got a good idea what that means, but I've convinced him it can wait until after the trial."

"I saw you with Roland earlier," said Elsa changing the subject, "but I didn't want him to know I was down here. I wanted us to spend this evening together. It seems such a long time since we've spent quality time together."

Suddenly, Jack and Elsa felt as close as they had before the incident on Walsh's boat when their lives were intertwined, and they were always together. They hugged and Jack kissed Elsa tenderly.

"I'll just take a quick shower before dinner," said Jack as they broke from their embrace and he went in the bathroom to turn on the water. He got undressed, and returned to the bathroom.

While Jack was in the shower, Elsa switched on the TV and tuned into the local news. A report on the Walsh trial followed the headline news item. The anchorman in the studio handed over to Dee Hamilton outside the courthouse. She had been reporting the trial since its start and gave regular evening updates of the day's events. She began her report by describing Simon Walsh's first day on the stand.

"Today Simon Walsh took the stand to give his version of the events that took place on his boat that led to the disappearance of Elsa Bartelli. Mr. Walsh testified that Miss Bartelli had tried to seduce him on his boat, but that things turned sour when he caught her trying to steal his wallet. He threatened her with the police and a scuffle ensued, which ended in her jumping overboard. Mr. Walsh confirmed he didn't know Miss Bartelli was a lap dancer or that she also worked as a prostitute. The defense still has to demonstrate that…"

Jack heard a loud crash in the living room, grabbed a towel and rushed out of the bathroom to find the cause of the commotion. He was dripping from head to toe, and looked a sorry sight as he rushed into the living area of the hotel room to find himself staring at a hole in the television screen.

"Did you hear what that sanctimonious bitch on the TV said about me?" Elsa didn't pause for a response from Jack, but carried on, full throttle. "OK. So, I'm an exotic dancer, but I'm not with a different man every night, and it certainly doesn't mean I'm a hooker. What sort of person do they think I am?"

"Slow down, Elsa. If you had waited until the end of the report before 'turning' the TV off, you'd have heard her say that the defense still has to prove that you were a prostitute."

"But what if my Gus and Jean hear of these accusations? It's bad enough that they think I'm dead. The only thing that's holding me together right now is my own self-respect, and the will not to let all of this get the better of me. Nobody has ever owned me nor will they ever. But you've managed to take that away from me now. Everyone thinks I'm some kind of tramp that can be bought for pin money."

"Please, don't get upset, Elsa...."

Jack didn't finish his sentence because Elsa slapped him sharply across the face and ran into the bedroom. At that moment, the doorbell rang. Jack grabbed his bathrobe from the bathroom before answering the door, but was still dripping wet when he opened the door. The bellboy gave Jack a funny look across the door threshold, and looked even more startled when he pushed the dinner trolley into the room and saw the damaged TV.

"I had an accident," said Jack quickly, "I'll pay for the TV in the morning." With that, Jack tipped the bellboy handsomely, and ushered him out of the room.

Jack walked into the bedroom to see Elsa lying face down on the bed, sobbing quietly. Jack sat on the side of the bed, and gently put his hand on her shoulder. "I'm truly sorry, Elsa. I didn't realize you'd get such a mauling in court."

Elsa lifted herself onto her elbows and brushed her hair from her face. "Well, they're right, aren't they? I did try to lure Walsh with the promise of sex, just like all of the other men we ripped off. I didn't actually have sex with them, but that's not really the point, is it? Maybe I'm no better than a hooker, and I've just been kidding myself that there's more to me than a good body."

"C'mon, Elsa! That's not true and you know it. Don't let a few lurid headlines from some media clown do this to you. The TV people are just trying to cash in on your background because it's an astonishing story they can exploit. You know your true worth as a person as I do, otherwise I wouldn't feel the way I do about you."

"Nothing really changes between us, does it? Even now, knowing how depressed I am and how I feel about you, you can't tell me that you love me. Now would be a really good time to tell me, if you mean it."

"What's so important about saying the obvious, you know how I feel," Jack replied insensitively. "OK. I love you!"

"That's not how I wanted you to say it, so let's just forget it, Jack. You were right my coming down here was a bad idea because you clearly don't give a shit about what I'm going through or how this business is affecting us. I don't think any amount of money is worth all of this."

"I never considered this happening, probably because I know you for who you are. People will always think the worst, its human nature, but the people who know you, know your worth." Jack hugged Elsa, trying to shield her from the accusations of the outside world.

They lay silently on the bed for a few minutes and Jack asked Elsa if she felt better. Elsa nodded, and Jack suggested they eat the dinner before it got cold.

Elsa was now even more depressed than she was before flying to Miami. Her joy at the thought of seeing Jack again was quickly dissipated by his continual hunger for money and unfeeling platitude of love. She was now beginning to question his true feelings for her and whether she was just the means for him to get rich. Words of love aren't always easy and she'd been waiting so long for him to tell her he loved her. Now he'd callously taken that dream away from her, because anything he said in future would be marred by his words and actions in a cold hotel room in Miami.

Jack had felt under pressure from Elsa, and realized that by not comforting her in the way she wanted, he was putting a big strain on their relationship. But he couldn't help himself. He knew that Elsa wanted them to settle down and live together, but Jack couldn't picture himself in a conventional relationship and with just one woman. She was his greatest passion, but he still felt he needed to cling on to his freedom. The cracks in their relationship were getting deeper.

The next morning, Jack drove Elsa to the airport to catch a plane back to Boston. They didn't talk much on their trip to the airport and Jack felt distant and that something between them had died in the hotel room.

"Give it time," he thought. "Things will get back to normal when we get the money."

His mantra was wearing a bit thin, even to himself.

21:

SELF-DESTRUCTION

It was now Bantry's turn to cross-examine Walsh. He was keen to put him under pressure, but kept reminding himself that he would have to build his argument slowly and meticulously to avoid being obvious in his lead up to the killer question. This case had blown up to be something bigger than he had ever anticipated; it was now firmly in the public spotlight, and that meant that a successful prosecution could do a lot to further his career. Despite a slight nervousness, which was unusual, he felt destiny was taking a hand.

"Please remember, Mr. Walsh, that you are still under oath," he began as he walked up to the witness box. Bantry's style was far more animated than that of his defense colleague and he would often walk over to a witness for a face-to-face confrontation, then pull away in mock amazement at an obtuse answer, or show disbelief of the response given. He would also walk over to the jury from time to time, and make eye contact with individuals when trying to emphasize a point. He also hoped that establishing a personal rapport with the jurors would help in reinforcing his closing argument at the end of the trial.

"We've heard a great deal about the moral character — or should I say the lack of moral character? — of Miss Bartelli. What was your opinion of her, Mr. Walsh?"

"Initially, I didn't have any opinion of her as a person. As I said earlier, she appeared to be a normal tourist relaxing on vacation, and certainly didn't look like she was soliciting. I didn't have any reason to think she was anything other than the impression her appearance gave."

"Well, I accept that statement wholeheartedly, because I know you are somewhat of an authority on hookers." A ripple of laughter went around the courtroom.

"Objection!" Tavistock shouted. "The prosecution is trying to make capital from cheap innuendo at my client's expense."

"I agree Mr. Tavistock," Judge Hyam replied. "Mr. Bantry, let me remind you that this is a court of law, and, therefore, your questions must be concise and to the point and most of all, pertinent to the case. Unsubstantiated attempts to ridicule the witness will not be tolerated. Do you understand, Mr. Bantry?"

"Yes, I apologize, Your Honor," said Bantry respectfully.

Turning to Walsh, he asked, "What was your intention when you offered to take Miss Bartelli out on your boat?"

Walsh sat quietly for a moment trying to formulate an answer that would be acceptable to the jury and also to his wife. "As I said earlier, it was the last day of her vacation and I wanted to give her something to remember," said Walsh, which was followed by further laughter in the courtroom. Hyam brought down his gavel sharply and called for quiet. Walsh continued, "When I met Miss Bartelli, we seemed to strike up an instant rapport. I was immediately attracted to her, and I also wanted to prolong our meeting. It seemed a nice idea to take her out to the reef and then cruise along the coast."

"Yes, but what was your intention in doing that?" Bantry persisted.

"I didn't have any specific intention or objective behind the invitation, if that's what you mean. I didn't need to go on another fishing trip and wanted to spend a little more time with her. Having the company of someone I could get to know and relax with seemed a more enjoyable way of spending the afternoon on my boat than going out alone."

"So your intentions were not completely benevolent; to end her vacation on a high note, as you said yesterday?"

"Yes, I did sympathize with her situation, but that was not the only reason I asked her out. She was attractive and interesting, and we got on well together in the bar."

"That's not what I meant, so I'll be clearer. Did you have any intentions of a sexual nature toward Miss Bartelli? Did you want to express yourself more openly when you got her alone on your boat and far enough out to sea to act on them without attracting unwanted attention?"

"I wouldn't do what you're suggesting."

"OK. If that's the case, give me a better explanation of your motives."

"To be honest I didn't know what would happen when we got out to sea. I thought that if we continued to get on well together, I'd take her out to dinner that evening. She had made arrangements with her sister, but I thought I could gate-crash and take them both out." Walsh had gone over that line a hundred times, and still couldn't make it sound convincing.

"But you're a married man, Mr. Walsh."

"For God's sake I was only contemplating dinner; don't tell me that having dinner with someone of the opposite sex automatically turns you into an adulterer."

A slight ripple of laughter went around the court again, to Bantry's annoyance, as he was on the receiving end of the gibe.

"No, Mr. Walsh, I can confirm that I often have dinner with female colleagues without any sexual connotations; the difference being, of course, that they are friends I have known for some time, and not people I have just picked up in a bar. Was there a difference between your relationship with Miss Bartelli and with the prostitutes you admit to have been with? She agreed to go only a few minutes after first meeting you, which is about the length of time it takes to make a transaction on the street. Apart from the fact that there was no financial transaction at the start, it was a normal pickup. Was that your perception?"

"Objection, Your Honor! Mr. Bantry is trying to harass the witness," Tavistock interjected.

"Objection overruled, Mr. Tavistock," Judge Hyam replied. "I can understand the importance of ascertaining what Mr. Walsh's first impressions of Miss Bartelli were, his attitude toward her and if he expected their relationship to become intimate."

"Well, Mr. Walsh?" Bantry asked.

"As I said earlier, she didn't look or act like a hooker. Yes, she gave off a sexy persona because of her striking appearance, but didn't flaunt it in a cheap way. She was well dressed and had a cultured manner, which is not evident with street girls. I guess in the back of my mind, I may have hoped we could become intimate, but not in the way she flaunted herself on the boat."

"But I would have thought that you would be quite used to the brazen behavior of women in view of your history."

"Not taking her for a hooker at the start, I guess she threw me off balance," Walsh replied, annoyed at Bantry's constant references to his past relationships with prostitutes.

"You agree that she was a sophisticated woman and must have known you were a wealthy man?"

"Yes."

"Then, why would she be satisfied with the small change in your wallet when she could have had far more by trying to develop a deeper, more meaningful relationship with you? You said yourself that she was obviously intelligent, so surely she wouldn't have sold herself so cheaply."

"I can't answer for her motives or actions," Walsh replied. This was a response that Tavistock hammered home to deal with Elsa's irrational behavior.

"Quite so, but it's a mystery, especially when you consider the size of her bank balance at that time." Bantry walked over to his table and picked up a piece of paper and then showed it to the jury. "This is the bank statement of Miss Bartelli's finances at the end of the month she disappeared. It shows that she had $135,000 in her account at that time. So I ask you again why she would travel all the way down to Florida for the few hundred bucks you carry in your wallet."

"I don't know. Maybe she planned a quiet drink and just decided to take a chance when the opportunity arose."

"OK, Mr. Walsh. We had better move on. I would like this bank statement and other documents to be included as evidence as they show Miss Bartelli's assets at the time of her disappearance were worth more than $200,000."

Bantry then turned to Judge Hyam, and explained that blood and hair samples had been taken from the deck of Walsh's boat, and a DNA match was found with hair samples from Elsa Bartelli's hairbrush. Bantry went back to his table and exchanged the bank statement for another piece of paper, which he held up in front of Walsh.

"This is the summary of a forensic report of tests on blood and hair samples taken from your boat. Firstly, the blood samples taken from the deck of your boat proved to be from Miss Bartelli. Can you explain how the blood got there?"

Walsh's face colored, and he became a little restless as he shifted uneasily on his seat.

"She must have hurt herself in the scuffle we had when I found her with my wallet."

"A scuffle sounds like a slight fracas without any real violence. But the samples taken from the deck of your boat indicate that she must have landed on it very hard. She may have fallen to the deck, possibly after being knocked down by you. Is that what happened, Mr. Walsh?"

"I don't know....it all happened so quickly. She may have fallen onto the deck, but I certainly didn't knock her down."

"Well, if she was bleeding as a result of your fight, I would have assumed that you would have had blood on your clothes.

That is, unless you held her at arm's length during the 'scuffle'. Did you have blood on your clothes, Mr. Walsh?"

"I didn't have any bloodstains on my clothes. In fact, I wasn't aware that she was bleeding."

"The bloodstains were found on the starboard side of the boat next to the handrail in sufficient quantities to leave a large stain. Did she fall by the handrail?"

"I've already told you that I don't know," Walsh stammered.

"Some strands of hair were also found, but nearer to the middle of the deck. These hair samples were also from Miss Bartelli. Can you explain that, Mr. Walsh?"

"No, I can't, because I can't remember the way things happened in any real detail," Walsh replied.

Play dumb, he thought, and limit the damage of Bantry's cross-examination by saying as little as possible. He looked anxiously toward Tavistock, trying to get some comfort or approval of his performance. Tavistock for his part was worried that Walsh was unable to give a good explanation of the bloodstains. Rather than act dumb, he was supposed to say that they both fell hard onto the deck during their fight, and that she landed underneath him.

"The locations of the hair and blood samples indicate that they weren't produced by a scuffle, but that the fight between you and Elsa was intense. Did you try and force yourself on her?" Bantry asked.

"I've already told you; it was she who started with the sexual overtures, not me."

"The forensic evidence does not support your explanation. The jury will have to decide whether or not they believe you."

Bantry continued, "When Miss Bartelli fell overboard, you were reluctant to try and rescue her in case she eluded you and got back into the boat while you were still in the water. Is that correct, Mr. Walsh?"

"Yes."

"But there must have been other measures you could have taken to try and rescue her without having to go into the water. Why didn't you throw her a safety line or a life saver?"

"I couldn't see her to throw her a lifeline. Besides, everything happened so fast I couldn't think straight."

"That seems to be your answer for everything, Mr. Walsh. Let's be clear about the sequence of events. You saw Miss Bartelli go overboard, and when you looked over the side, you didn't see any sign of her resurfacing."

"No."

"How long did you look for her?"

"It seemed a long time. I went to both sides of the boat to try and catch sight of her."

"Was the sea rough or were conditions such that it would have been difficult to see her floating in the water?"

"No."

"Well, there can only be one of two explanations, Mr. Walsh. Either she was dead when she fell into the water, or you didn't spend any time looking for her, and simply, left her where she fell overboard. Which was it, Mr. Walsh?"

"I've already told you what happened. I don't know why I couldn't see her in the water! The shock of the impact with the water may have knocked her unconscious. How should I know?"

"You have already testified that you did not call the coastguard to report the incident?"

"Yes."

"Why couldn't you have reported your position? The coastguard might have had a boat in the area and sent out assistance to help find Miss Bartelli? Tell the court why you didn't call the coastguard."

"How many times do I have to repeat myself? I wasn't thinking straight," Walsh stammered, desperate to find something to say that could mitigate the heartless action of leaving his victim in the sea.

"Miss Bartelli's disappearance would have been very convenient for you. After all, she might have reported your attack to the police after your return to the marina."

Walsh shook his head, disagreeing with the implication behind Bantry's question.

"I know you can't answer that, Mr. Walsh, but tell me this. Did you think to report the incident to anyone at the marina when you got back?"

"No."

"You didn't tell anyone about Miss Bartellis's accident. What were you trying to cover up?"

"I've already said that by this time, I was frightened that I would be accused of harming her."

"Well, you're right in that respect. Do you own a gun, Mr. Walsh?"

"Yes, I do."

"Is this the gun?" Bantry asked, handing a gun in a polythene bag to Walsh.

"I think it is. It's certainly the same model," Walsh replied.

"I can tell you that it is your gun and that we have checked records to confirm it's registered to you." Bantry turned to the jury. "This gun was found at Mr. Walsh's home shortly after his arrest, and forensic tests confirm that it had been fired recently. Did you have this gun on your boat the day you met Miss Bartelli?" Bantry asked, turning back to Walsh.

"I don't know, I can't remember."

"You don't seem to be able to remember much, do you Mr. Walsh?" said Bantry sarcastically. Walsh hated being humiliated in this way and mentally braced himself as Bantry continued, "Do you normally take the gun with you on vacation?"

"I don't consciously carry it with me everywhere. I originally bought it after hearing about burglaries in my apartment building."

"That's strange, as your wife told the police that you always took the gun to Florida with you after your encounter with a vagrant sleeping on your boat. I'll ask you again, Mr. Walsh, did you have your gun with you the afternoon you took Miss Bartelli out on your boat?"

"Yes, I did, but I didn't shoot her!"

"You're jumping ahead of me, Mr. Walsh," said Bantry, turning to the jury and smiling at them knowingly. "Let's examine the facts that have been established so far. You claim Miss Bartelli tried to seduce you, but on finding her with your wallet, a scuffle ensued in which she may or may not have fallen on the deck. Samples of hair and blood found on your boat were from Miss Bartelli. Hair samples in the middle of the deck indicate that she fell during your fight. Blood stains on the starboard side of the deck show that she was injured in that area. Finally, you confirm that there were no bloodstains on your clothing, indicating she was some distance away from you when the injury occurred."

Bantry paused to let the jury digest the thread running through his brief summary of Walsh's fight with Elsa. "I think you're right Mr. Walsh, the only conclusion that I can draw from these facts is that you tried to force yourself on the unfortunate, innocent Miss Bartelli, and when she tried to escape your crude advances, you shot her."

"That's not true!" Walsh shouted, panicking because Bantry had closely described actual events. "You've got everything twisted. Elsa Bartelli was not an unfortunate, innocent woman; she was a cockteaser on the make and deserved what she got."

There was an audible gasp around the court in response to Walsh's outburst, which made him pause and reconsider what he had just said. "I wasn't talking about the shooting; I was talking about her drowning." This time the response from the spectators was even more pointed as an even louder buzz went around the court. Tavistock sat with his head in his hands, feeling utterly crushed by his client's outbursts.

Judge Hyam brought down his gavel sharply and once again asked for quiet in the courtroom. It took a few seconds for the low drone to subside. He turned to Bantry signaling him to continue.

"That's all, Your Honor," said Bantry.

"Thank you, Mr. Walsh. No more questions."

Bridget Walsh was stunned, like the rest of the court, by her husband's final statement. A hollow feeling had developed in the pit of her stomach, and she felt it radiating outward, numbing the rest of her body. Her worst fears were suddenly realized. The initial shock she felt was gradually replaced by nausea when she had to admit to herself that she had been living with a man without a shred of common human decency. Impulsively, she wanted to leave the courtroom as quickly as she could to distance herself from the testimony she had just heard. Without a glance to her husband, she rose from her seat close to the aisle, and turned toward the rear of the courtroom. Hurrying to the exit, she pushed one of the courtroom doors open, and took a deep lungful of cool air, and started to compose herself.

As she turned to the lobby to leave the court building a news reporter, who must have seen her hurried exit from the courtroom, intercepted her. "Mrs. Walsh, can I have your reaction to your husband's testimony," the eager journalist asked.

"What do you think? Go away and stop asking me stupid questions!" she shouted at him. She picked up her speed but the reporter was not going to be put off, as he followed and cut off her exit.

"But, Mrs. Walsh, you must have felt something after hearing what your husband said about Elsa deserving what she got."

"Have you got no sense of decency, or is everyone fair game for your cheap rag?" Bridget hissed, and with that, she briskly brushed the reporter aside before he could deliver a follow-up question, and strode toward the building exit without hesitation.

Jack had seen the reporter follow Bridget out of the courtroom, and had tailed them both to see how she would handle being harassed. She had recovered quickly from what must have been a massive blow to her own ego, if not to her emotions, and dealt with the reporter effectively. A very determined woman thought Jack making a mental note not to underestimate her in their future negotiations.

When he returned to the courtroom, Jack found Tavistock questioning Walsh, reworking some of his earlier testimony in an attempt to repair some of the damage he had inflicted upon himself. Jack knew his attorney could not undo the impact of those final statements on the minds of the jury. Tavistock was also aware that the damage of Walsh's testimony could lead to a guilty verdict, and was already thinking about grounds for appeal. In an act of self-destruction, Walsh had undone all of Tavistock's hard work.

22:

GOODBYE, AL

Al Ferrino had heard about Walsh's faux pas of the previous day and was expecting a call from Jack Cates. The voice he heard on the other end of the line was unfamiliar.

"Hello, Mr. Ferrino! My name is Roland Bannister. How are you?"

"How do you know me, and who the hell are you?" Al replied, agitated at getting a call from a stranger.

"I'm sorry, Mr. Ferrino. Let me explain. I'm a business associate of Jack Cates, who has asked me to contact you now that a Walsh conviction seems certain. Jack has asked me to make arrangements for the delivery of your money before the end of the trial."

"You've got my 150 grand, then?"

Bannister paused for a second, thinking that Ferrino had as much chance of winning the lottery as getting his hands on that amount of money. "Do you think I'm going to walk through the streets of New York carrying that kind of money?" he replied a little aggressively. "Besides, it's quite a large package that I've put in a safe place, so we need to make arrangements for you to collect it."

"OK," said Al, who hadn't thought about the volume of such a large amount of money, and was suddenly at a loss for words. Neither had he thought through the manner in which the money would be handed over. Bannister's compliance was unexpected, as Jack played hardnose the last time they spoke, and he felt more than a little relieved he wouldn't have to face Jack again.

"I can come over to your house, or......."

"No, there's no need for that," Al interjected. "The neighborhood is not so good and I don't want anyone seeing you make the delivery. I want to pay it straight into a new bank account."

Al didn't want his long-suffering wife to know about the source of the money as despite their desperate financial circumstance, she would have nothing to do with a blackmailer's money. Al and his wife had been married for 25 years, and had very little to show for their time together. They didn't own their home, nor did they have any children or a pension fund. Al had worked spasmodically, flitting from one dead-end job to another before finally settling down to his job at the marina. His gambling habit made it impossible for them to save anything from their meagre resources. Al decided that once he got this money, they would buy a home in a decent area, and use the balance as an investment to fall back on, if necessary, and enjoy their retirement.

"Can we meet at midday during your lunch break? You can take the money straight to whatever bank you like."

"I can meet you between 1 and 2," Al replied.

"Come over to my hotel and we can finish the deal," Bannister suggested.

"No, I don't want to meet in your hotel room; I want us to meet in a public place."

"That's a little disappointing, Al. I've been very open and friendly with you, and I thought we were getting on very well."

"We can socialize as much as you like after the money's in the bank, but 'til then it's strictly business."

"Well, where shall we meet?"

"There's an Irish bar in Brickell, which isn't too far from the marina. Meet me there at 1:10."

"OK," Bannister agreed, "but how will I recognize you?"

"I'll be sitting in the right-hand corner booth at the rear of the bar," Al replied curtly, then put the phone back on its receiver.

Al was amazed at how easy it all was, and was beginning to regret he hadn't asked for more money.

"Don't be greedy," he thought.

It was likely what he was getting was small compared to what Jack expected to get out of Walsh. Surely, he and Bannister wouldn't take any unnecessary chances for a measly 150 grand.

When Roland Bannister entered the Irish bar, he briefly perused the decor and tried to absorb the ambience of the place. He walked over to the barman and ordered a brandy, pointing to the right-hand corner booth described by Al. The barman was about to explain that there was no waiter service in the bar as Roland strode away, leaving the barman with his mouth hanging open. Roland's training and experience as a lawyer had taught him to prepare a case meticulously, and try to catch the opposition off guard. He thought his early arrival would unsettle Al, particularly if this was his own watering hole, which he had probably selected so as to be in familiar surroundings when closing the deal.

The disgruntled barman delivered the brandy to the booth and set it down loudly in front of Roland, who looked up at him, smiled politely, and nodded in gratitude. The barman scowled at not receiving a tip and returned to the bar. Roland picked up the glass and took a sip of the brandy, but his face creased immediately as the coarseness of the liquor hit the back of his throat. He pushed the glass away, realizing that he should have known better than to expect a quality brandy in this type of bar. He briefly looked around and saw, away from the booths, it was a typical watering hole for tourists. It was also a draw for locals working in the area, who would probably crowd the bar. He wondered how many of the regulars in this bar would frequent the Blue Cockatoo.

Still absorbing the atmosphere of the place, Roland noticed a short stocky man enter the bar and collect a beer from the counter. The man looked inquisitively at the booth and took a few tentative steps in its direction, not knowing what to expect. Roland stood up and signaled to the man to join him and as the stranger approached, he held out his hand, saying "Hello, Al!"

Al took his hand, making a weak handshake and moved into the seat opposite. "Have you got the money?" he asked immediately.

"Slow down, Al. Have you got any idea how big a $150,000 package broken down into denominations of hundreds, fifties and twenties is? I would look conspicuous bringing such a package in here and you would spend the next month explaining to people what was in the package I handed over."

"Don't try and be clever." Al shrugged, bemused by the slick appearance of Bannister and the way words just seemed to roll off his tongue. "We agreed that you would hand over the money here. I can handle any awkward questions, so what's the problem?"

"Listen, I'm trying to do what's safest and best for both of us. I couldn't hand you a large package in this joint without drawing attention to ourselves. I've got the money stashed in a safe place just waiting for you to go and pick it up."

"So where is it?" Al asked impatiently.

"I've put the money in a travel bag in one of the baggage lockers at the train station and here's the key," said Roland, producing a shiny metal object from the inside pocket of his jacket, and handing it to Al. "The locker number is 177, which is on the tab attached to the key. The station lobby is wide open and you can collect the bag in your own time without looking conspicuous."

"The train station's at least 10 blocks away," Al moaned, taking the key from Bannister.

"I can drive you there if you want."

"No. It's OK. I'll make my own way there," Al replied, and with that, he stood up and left the bar with his beer virtually untouched.

Al pondered on when to collect the money as he walked out of the bar, but by the time he hit the street he had decided to collect it straight away. He hailed a taxi, and instructed the driver to take him to Miami Central Station as he got into the cab. He still had the locker key in his hand and looked down at it, smiling to himself and thinking about the change this money would bring to his and Nora's lives. Before buying a house, he would put the money in a high interest account for a few years, let it accrue interest, and then tell Nora that he had made some stock-market investments that had grown beyond all expectations.

The cab driver pulled up outside the entrance to Miami Central Station and Al paid the fare, without adding a tip. He may have been expecting to come into a large amount of money, but he wasn't a generous man and history showed he was unlikely to change. Suspicious of everything, he cautiously entered the station to get his bearings. The main lobby was large and had overhead signs giving directions to different parts of the complex including the baggage lockers, which were signed. Their location in an ante lobby on the left-hand side of the wide spread of departure gates to train platforms was within easy reach.

Al followed the sign and started hurrying, but then slowed his pace to avoid drawing unwanted attention from commuters which could alert one of Bannister's flunkeys. Casually he surveyed the numbers on the lockers. The lockers were on the two opposing walls of the ante chamber offering a total of 500 storage boxes. They were arranged in five rows on each wall, numbered in increments of 50 between 1 and 250, and 251 to 500. He couldn't concentrate because the thought of having such a large amount of money was now becoming a reality to him.

Al had never seen 150 grand in one bundle and in his eagerness to get his hands on the money he couldn't maintain his casual pace, rushing to scan the lockers closest to him from their nearest edge. Locker number 101 began the middle row and he hurried forward counting locker numbers.... 151, 160, 165, 175.........177 on the row below it. The tension mounted as he got closer to the right box and when he reached 177 moisture covered his face. The locker looked the same as all the others in the array but he gazed at it, catching his breath and trying to imagine the stash of money on the other side of the door.

He still clutched the key that Bannister had given him, and he inserted it into the door lock, turned it anti-clockwise and slowly opened the door. Inside the locker was a cheap brown-and-cream, plastic carryall, zipped tight. Al unzipped the carryall and put his hand inside to feel its contents. The bag held a paper parcel wrapped with string. He reached for a penknife in his pocket, pulled out the blade, and thrust it into the package. Ripping the wrapping in an upward direction, he made an opening of about six inches. Eagerly he stuck his hand through the opening and felt bundles of money inside the parcel. He searched for the edge of a bill, grabbed it and pulled his hand free. Al looked at the note to see a blank sheet of paper cut into the shape of a dollar bill. He thrust his hand into the package again to pull out a handful of bills, and found they were all blank sheets of paper.

The discovery meant he had been set up and was being observed by someone who probably had a contract to hurt or even kill him. His pulse started to race, he got hot and perspiration appeared on his face. People began looking at him as he stood dumbfoundedly next to the barrage of lockers holding scraps of paper and he decided to get out of the station as quickly as he could. He let the pieces of bill-shaped paper drop from his hand, sheathed the penknife, put it in his pocket, and headed for the main lobby. Al was unaware of commuters parting as he approached them, thinking only of finding the exit signs.

Instinctively, he knew his only chance of survival was to get away from the station and blend with the people going about their everyday business on the street. If someone was stalking him, they would have identified him as he went to collect the money from the locker. Reaching the main lobby, he headed for the nearest exit, continually looking around to see if he was being followed. He would have liked to run out of the station, but that would have attracted more attention, and his physical condition wouldn't allow him to run for more than a minute or two. As he approached the exit doors, Al's anxiety began to be gradually replaced by a deep sense of relief. The automatic doors opened and he skipped over the threshold, again turning to see if he was being followed. No one appeared to be taking any interest in him and he began to wonder if Bannister's intent was simply to scare him. The realization he was on the wrong end of Bannister's trick had scared him, but instead of running away, he would make the double crosser pay by asking for more money.

Al started walking up the service road to the taxi rank, and was stopped in his tracks by someone calling his name from the direction of the exit he had just passed through. He turned to see a man standing by the automatic doors who was holding the brown-and-cream carryall aloft, and waving him back. The anxiety flooded back, he became flushed and started to run toward the taxi rank, turning intermittently to see the man slowly following him. The combination of his panic and the sudden exertion made him breathe heavily, and he felt as if his heart was going to burst out of his chest. He turned back and ran straight into a man walking in the opposite direction toward the station, knocking him to the ground. The shock of the collision made Al step backward, rubbing his head, which was ringing from the force of the impact. Looking more closely at the man he had just knocked over, he could see he was blind, wearing dark glasses and with a white telescopic walking stick, which had retracted. He apologized to the blind man who held out his hand in a gesture for Al to help him up. Nervously, Al looked toward the station to see the man with the carryall still walking slowly up the service road.

"He won't do anything with witnesses around," Al thought, and he reached out to grab the outstretched hand of the blind man.

He was big and heavy, and Al strained himself even further pulling him up to his feet. Rising unsteadily, the blind man groped for an arm to try and stabilize himself, but as the heads of the two men became level, Al felt a sharp pain on the left side of his chest. His legs went weak and suddenly could no longer support him, but the blind man who towered above him when standing up straight, strongly held Al upright to prevent him collapsing onto the pavement. Al stared up at the face of the blind man through a blurred haze, and the last image he saw before dying was the parting of the man's lips into a broad smile. With perfect timing, the man launched Al into the road just in front of an oncoming car that was driving toward the train station. The sickening thud of Al's body striking the front, nearside corner of the car made the driver stand hard on his brakes. Even though the car was traveling slowly, it managed to drag Al's body about 15 feet before coming to a halt. The driver scrambled from his car, and rushed to the front of it, to see the mess he had made of the man he had hit, screaming to the passenger that he hadn't seen him.

"That blind-man trick never fails, Frank," said Lou, congratulating his partner as they drove downtown. "Always finding the heart with the steel pin in the stick... it's amazing. Man, you're an artist!"

"Never mind that, Lou. Did you clean up?"

"Yeah. Of course, I did. Got the carryall, cleaned the locker, closed it and returned the key. You know I'm reliable. There are no loose ends."

"OK. Step on the gas! I'm hungry."

23:

VERDICT

Bantry began his summing up by painting Elsa Bartelli as an innocent woman trapped on a boat with a man prepared to do anything to have sex with her. Maybe she was a lap dancer, but that didn't mean she shouldn't be treated with the same dignity and respect as any other woman, or that she didn't deserve the same protection from the law.

He concluded by saying, "The precise details of Elsa's death will never be known to anyone but Simon Walsh. But he fabricated a story of her trying to seduce him for the paltry amount of money in his wallet, and only showed us the true nature of his feelings toward women at the end of his testimony stating, she 'deserved what she got'."

Bantry paused, letting the jurors remember Walsh's performance on the stand. "There is sufficient evidence of Elsa putting up a strenuous fight, but to no avail. Walsh ruthlessly murdered her to cover up his assault on her body, and concocted a ridiculous story when he was arrested. Don't forget he failed to report her disappearance when he returned to the marina and he failed to call the coastguard for help when he was out at sea. Why? What was he trying to hide? He was hoping his crime would go undetected and that Elsa would just become another missing person statistic. Members of the jury, I ask you to give Elsa the justice she deserves, and find this man guilty of murder."

Tavistock had a far more difficult task in trying to convince the jury of Walsh's innocence. He tried to portray Walsh as a victim caught up in circumstances beyond his control. "Don't judge the moral character of the defendant. He is being tried for murder, not for his sexual habits or preferences. The only crime he is guilty of is not reporting the incident to the authorities when it happened or after he had returned to the marina. But surely you can understand his frame of mind at the time and the pressure he must have been under to keep his wife, family and friends from finding out about the incident. He is guilty of gross misjudgment and putting his own interests ahead of his unfortunate passenger, but he is not guilty of murder."

Jack scrutinized the jury as Tavistock was trying to mitigate the callousness of his client's actions. As he studied the faces of the jury members, he was pleased to see that they all had impassive expressions, and were clearly not empathizing with what was being said. He also noticed that Bridget Walsh was not in the courtroom, which he thought might also be picked up by the keener members of the jury.

Following Tavistock's closing argument, Judge Hyam turned to the jury to instruct them on the points of law that they should consider in coming to their verdict. "Members of the jury," he began, "you will have to decide on whether Simon Walsh took Elsa Bartelli aboard his boat to compromise her sexually, and ended up killing her after he assaulted her, or that he was an innocent victim of a petty crime that resulted in tragic consequences. The office of the District Attorney has brought a homicide charge against him; however, the testimony of Mr. Walsh and others has shown that the cause of Miss Bartelli's death could have been due to any one of a number of different scenarios leading to her jumping off his boat or being thrown from it. Her body has not been found, so there's no physical evidence that she is in fact dead."

"The true circumstances of her disappearance may never be fully understood as there were no independent witnesses to the events that took place, and clearly Mr. Walsh's testimony to the police was aimed at protecting himself from prosecution, which has now taken place. You will have to judge the reliability of his testimony. In the same way, you must agree on the real motive of Miss Bartelli going out to sea with Mr. Walsh."

The judge took a sip of water, and continued, "If Mr. Walsh did murder Elsa Bartelli, clearly, it was not a premeditated act, as they had only met that afternoon. If you believe that he could have helped her but left her to die so as to cover up his attempted or actual rape, you must find him guilty of second-degree murder. On the other hand, if you feel he was provoked by her actions on the boat, and the ensuing fight with Miss Bartelli resulted in her accidental death, you must find him not guilty of murder, but guilty of manslaughter. Finally, if you believe his account of Miss Bartelli jumping overboard of her own volition, and that he was unable to help her get back onto the boat, you must find him innocent. If that is the case, charges may be brought against him later, for failing to call for help, and to report the incident."

"Remember that collectively you should come to a guilty verdict when you all firmly believe that the defendant committed murder or manslaughter. If you cannot all agree on a verdict, a majority verdict must be presented." Hyam paused to let the members of the jury process the information they had just been given. "Is that clear?" he finally asked and glanced from one jury member to the other for confirmation. They all nodded in agreement. "When you go into the jury room, the first thing you must do is to choose a foreman who will deliver your verdict to the court."

The members of the jury stood up, and then filed out of the courtroom. Judge Hyam adjourned the court proceedings until the jury was ready to deliver its verdict. It was just past 3:00 in the afternoon and Jack thought he'd grab a quick drink at the bar at the end of the block before going back to the hotel to call Bannister to let him know the jury was out.

While Jack was sat at the bar with a bottle of Bud to his mouth, James Bantry sidled up beside him, and slapped him on the back.

187

"I think I'll join you, Jack; it's been a difficult trial, and I need resuscitation."

Jack nodded and signaled the barman for service. Bantry ordered a whiskey sour and Jack asked that the drink be put on his tab. During the trial, the two men had become well-acquainred as they were both in the habit of going into the bar at the end of each day in court. Bantry had seen Jack's daily attendance, and knew he was Elsa's partner. He found he was able to paint a clearer picture of her through talking to him.

"How long do you think they'll be out?" Jack asked.

"It's difficult to say. We both know that Walsh is a lying, two-faced bastard, but it depends on what the jury made of him. Initially, the women will have been prejudiced against Elsa, having read all of the sordid details printed in the press before the trial. Luckily, Walsh didn't do himself any favors with his testimony. Because of that, I feel quietly confident."

"The judge gave the jury too many options. Do you think that will confuse them?"

"No, the choices are fairly straightforward, and surely, no one can really believe Walsh's ridiculous story of Elsa jumping overboard to escape. I don't know how Tavistock let him come into court with that yarn."

"Maybe they couldn't construe any other plausible reason for her going overboard without pointing the finger at Walsh," Jack answered. "Do you think the jury will be influenced by the fact that the police didn't find Elsa's body?"

"No, not necessarily, Jack. There are a number of precedents of murderers going down without the evidence of a corpse. Anyway, DNA put Elsa on the boat and eye-witness testimonies confirmed she wasn't on board when Walsh returned. The circumstantial evidence is overwhelming."

"I was looking at the jury while you and Tavistock made your closing remarks. They seemed far more receptive to your summing up than they did to his. Luckily, Walsh is so obnoxious that even Tavistock couldn't hide that fact."

"I know, Jack, but murderers aren't convicted because they aren't nice people, but because they're guilty. Let's hope the jury is convinced of his guilt." With that, Bantry finished his drink, and bade Jack farewell.

On the way back to his hotel, Jack picked up the evening edition of the *Miami Herald*. He felt a bit tired and the day had proven to be a little anti-climactic after the fireworks of Walsh's testimony the previous day. He had thought about the trial almost to the exclusion of everything and everyone else. Bantry could have injected a bit more 'fire and brimstone' into his closing remarks, heralding old-world values for the respect of women. Jack thought that he had been too restrained in his condemnation of Walsh's attitude to women, and had missed the opportunity to emphasize the negative statements Walsh made when giving evidence. Bantry should have tried to eradicate any last vestiges of doubt about Walsh's guilt that might still be lingering in some of the jurors' minds. He put Bantry's lackluster performance down to overconfidence.

At the hotel, Jack ordered coffee and sandwiches to be sent up to his room and decided he would stay in rather than go out on the town. There would be plenty of time to celebrate after the guilty verdict was returned. Once inside his room, Jack dropped the paper on the bed and turned into the bathroom to take a shower. The bellboy came with his order while he was still in his dressing gown. Jack poured a cup of coffee and settled down on the bed to read the paper. Halfway through, he noticed a small article on the death of a local man at the railway station. He sat bolt upright when he read that the name of the man was Al Ferrino.

The newspaper report stated that Al had been killed in a road accident outside the station. Unaccountably, he had fallen in front of an oncoming car, and had incurred severe head injuries from which he died. There were no witnesses to the accident other than the car driver and his girlfriend. Both were traumatized by the incident and were unable to comment to the paper. The police did not suspect foul play, although they would be making a full investigation into the incident.

Jack dropped the paper and picked up his cell phone to call Gene Tanner.

"Hello! This is Detective Tanner."

"It's Jack Cates, Gene. How are things with you?"

"I'm fine, Jack; busy as always…. Well, you know what the job's like."

"I know, and in a strange way, sometimes I still miss it. Then I think of the freedom I have now. Tell me, Gene, have you closed the file on Walsh?"

"I still have a little involvement, but as you know the jury went out to consider the verdict today, so the case will be closed shortly one way or the other. Let's hope the bastard goes down for a long time."

"You and me both," Jack replied. "Talking of the Walsh trial, I just read an article in the *Herald* about the death of Al Ferrino. Wasn't he one of the witnesses?"

"Yes, Ferrino was a witness, but he didn't actually appear in court. His evidence was read out to corroborate the testimonies of the barman and the mechanic. He was a strange little man, very aggressive but genuinely concerned about Elsa."

"What happened to him?"

"He was hit by a guy bringing his girlfriend to the train station. Apparently, they were having an argument, and didn't see Ferrino until it was too late. No one knows what he was doing at the station. All we do know is that he was on his lunch break from the marina."

"It's ironic that the poor guy was killed by a car at a train station, but I guess stranger things can happen."

"I'm glad you can see the funny side, Jack. It first appeared to be a freakish incident because Ferrino fell awkwardly, hit his head on the grill of the car, and perforated his skull behind his left ear. He would have died instantly had he still been alive. What really killed him was a puncture wound below his chest that can't be related to any physical object on the car. The coroner thinks it could have been a stiletto, but the entry of the wound gives a rising trajectory up to the heart. If that's the case, Ferrino didn't step in front of the car, he was thrown into its path."

"But the paper said the police didn't think he died in suspicious circumstances."

"I know. That's because we haven't got a clue as to what happened. If the stiletto theory is true, it has all the hallmarks of a professional hit…. but for what reason? Al Ferrino had no underworld connections, so we're just keeping a low profile on the case until we can make a few enquiries. What's your interest?"

"I met him at Walsh's trial. We got talking over a drink and he did seem very concerned over Elsa, especially when I told him that she had been my girl. I can't believe he had any criminal connections; he just didn't seem the type."

"It's a mystery, Jack. But how are you bearing up now that the trial's nearly over?"

"To be honest, my emotions have dulled. I've been living without Elsa for such a long time that that my passion for revenge has now gone. I'll just be glad when it's all over and Walsh is behind bars."

"I couldn't have sat through the trial like you, Jack, listening to the way he treated Elsa on his boat. The man's a low life, and he will hopefully get what he deserves."

"Yeah, the case seems quite straightforward to me, although you never can tell with these things," Jack replied.

"I'm just glad I was able to get onto the case so quickly, and run the rat down. He won't be using his money to compromise any other unsuspecting woman in the future."

"He should be behind bars to protect the public, never mind what he did to Elsa. When I think of the way he manhandled her, I could kill him," said Jack with genuine passion, remembering how he found her in the sea.

"I'm sorry, Jack. I didn't mean to stir things up for you again. Look. I've got to go now. Let's get together after the trial. Bye."

"Yeah. See you, Gene," said Jack, cancelling the call.

Frank and Lou, he thought; Bannister had got his two tame gorillas to see Al off. Jack was pissed off about Al's murder, because it was an unnecessary risk to take at this stage of the trial, and because he knew he could have dissuaded him from carrying out his threat to go to the police. Oddly, he had grown fond of the grumpy motorboat attendant, who had provided the initial impetus to get the investigation into Elsa's disappearance off the ground. Jack was annoyed Roland had taken unilateral action. That was a good indication of his commitment to the partnership, and demonstrated that he would undertake any action he considered necessary without consultation. Bannister would have covered his own tracks to ensure nothing could be used to connect him to the murder, but Jack also knew he wouldn't go to the same lengths to protect his partners. If Jack hadn't felt uneasy about their partnership before, he did now.

Suddenly, he felt very tired. He threw the paper off the bed, took off his dressing gown, and crawled under the covers. He fell asleep without turning off the light, and slept deeply without dreaming until the shrill sound of the bedside phone woke him. After several rings he lifted the receiver and held it to his ear.

"Yeah. Who is it?"

"Wake up, Jack! It's showtime!" James Bantry answered. "The jury reached a decision late last night and they'll be delivering their verdict at 9:30 this morning."

"OK. I'll be there," Jack replied and put the phone down.

It was 8:00, and he had slept through from the previous evening. Clearly, some of his recent late-night carousing around Miami had taken its toll.

Jack had a front seat in the courtroom to hear the jury's verdict. The spectator's seats were full, with local and national reporters for both newspapers and television, as well as Jerry, the barman, and Bridget Walsh. There was the buzz of conversation in the visitor's galleries, but Tavistock and Walsh were not talking to each other; that could have been an indication that they were expecting the worst. Bantry and John Delaney were talking in a relaxed manner, giving the impression they were confident of the outcome.

The court usher called the court to order for the entrance of Judge Hyam. Silence followed and the judge took his position on the bench. Walsh was told to stand for the verdict; this he duly did with his attorney.

Turning to the foreman of the jury Hyam asked if they had reached a verdict.

"Yes, Your Honor," the foreman replied in a strong, clear voice.

The courtroom was still as Judge Hyam then asked, "Do you find the defendant guilty or not guilty of second-degree murder?"

"Not guilty, Your Honor," the foreman replied.

Walsh gave a smile of relief and looked across at Bridget, who remained impassive, not showing any sign of relief. The foreman's answer resulted in a subdued hum that circulated around the courtroom, and Hyam banged his gavel loudly, and repeatedly, to bring the court to order. He waited for complete silence before turning to the foreman again.

"Do you find the defendant guilty or not guilty of manslaughter?"

"Guilty, Your Honor" was the reply.

A quiet hum again rose from the courtroom as the spectators passed comment on their opinion of the verdict. Hyam again demanded silence before continuing.

"Are you all agreed on the verdict?"

"Yes, Your Honor," the foreman replied.

"The members of the jury have come to the only verdict they could have in the light of the evidence placed before them," Hyam observed. He turned to Walsh, and added, "I take comfort in the legal system and generally, the unerring fairness of the juries I have had the pleasure of presiding over. Simon Walsh, you have been found guilty of manslaughter. Do you have anything to say before sentence is passed?"

Walsh's earlier relief at the not-guilty verdict for murder was replaced with more than a little anxiety, but he was relieved to be facing a sentence for manslaughter, and not murder. He thought hard about what he could say to put the judge in a lenient frame of mind.

"I can only say how sorry I am about the loss of Ms. Bartelli, Your Honor."

Such a platitude was hollow, and that was recognized by everyone in the court. Hyam paused after Walsh had finished. Jack wasn't sure whether it was to see if Walsh had anything further to say, or if it was to summon his own thoughts. Jack was feeling dejected about the not guilty verdict for murder, and was apprehensive about the sentence that would be given to Walsh for manslaughter.

"It's nice to hear that you are sorry for the events that took place on your boat last summer," Hyam began, looking straight at Walsh, "but I am not convinced that the sentiment is genuine. Throughout this episode, you have shown that your instincts for your own survival have by far outweighed any concern you have for the welfare of others. There is sufficient evidence on record, preceding the events of this trial which confirms your intolerable and inexcusable attitude toward women and the appalling manner in which you have behaved toward them. I believe that women should be protected until you have had time to come to understand the error of your ways and can be trusted not to reoffend. The exact circumstances of Miss Bartelli's disappearance will never be known, but I am convinced that she would be here today if not for your conduct that afternoon, on your boat. For this reason, I sentence you to not less than 10, and no more than 20, years in prison," the judge pronounced.

The look of disbelief on Walsh's face was the first genuine emotion he had displayed throughout the whole of the trial. Tavistock began explaining the appeal procedure to him, but he was too shocked to take in what his attorney was saying. He stared at Bridget, who stood up, and left the courtroom with just a brief glance in his direction. Even Tavistock was surprised she didn't go over to console her husband.

Jack found it hard to contain the undiluted joy he felt on hearing the sentence, and imagined he would experience the same euphoria on hearing that he'd won the lottery. It might not have been quite the result he had been expecting, but 10 to 20 years would give him plenty of leverage in his forthcoming negotiations with Walsh.

Jack headed back to the hotel to check out, and on the way, decided to call Roland Bannister from a phone booth to give him the news.

"Time to celebrate, Roland! Walsh got between 10 and 20 years for manslaughter."

"It's not what we expected, but it's a good result, Jack. Now we can start working on his wife. I've asked Bantry to find out where he will be sent. It will probably be Florida State, which is a medium-security jail, where we can get the ball rolling."

"I don't know if you've noticed, Roland, but the ball has been rolling for some time now."

"Don't be touchy, Jack. You know what I mean. We've been given the green light, and now our success is in our own hands."

"Does that mean we shouldn't take risks?"

"Yes, of course, it does. We don't want to blow this deal now."

"Then why put Frank and Lou onto Al?"

Jack heard Roland take a sharp intake of breath on the other end of the line.

First Deceit

"This isn't something we should be discussing on the phone, and you know it. If we are going to see this thing through, there must be trust between us, Jack."

"Trust is a two-way thing, Roland. Don't forget that."

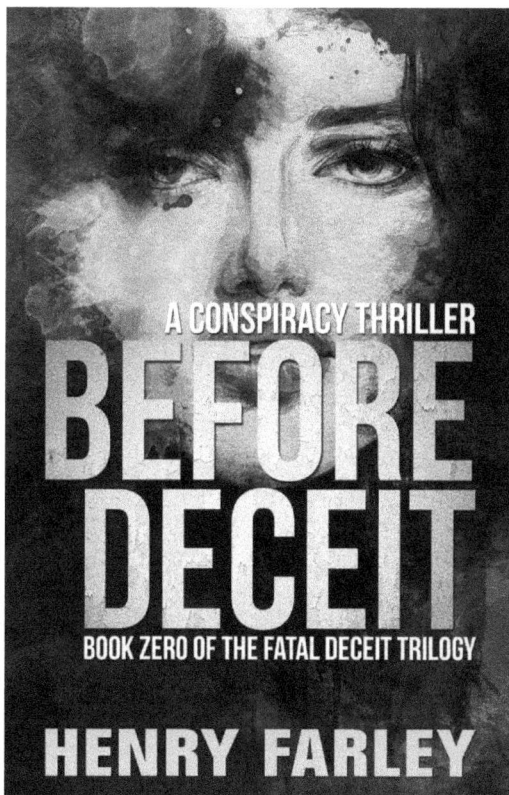

www.ingramcontent.com/pod-product-compliance
Lightning Source LLC
Chambersburg PA
CBHW022111210326
41521CB00028B/216